Copyright ©2019 by Isha Cogborn

All rights reserved. No part of this publication may be reproduced, transmitted or stored in any form or by any means without the written permission of the author except in the case of brief quotations.

The material in this publication is provided for information purposes only. Procedures, laws and regulations are constantly changing and the examples given are intended to be general guidelines only. This book is sold with the understanding that no one involved in this publication is attempting herein to render professional advice.

For information, interviews or bulk order discounts, contact isha@EpiphanyInstitute.com

Published in the United States by Epiphany Institute.
www.EpiphanyInstitute.com

ISBN: 978-1-7332721-0-0
Library of Congress Control Number: 2019947860

Cover design and layout by Riddick Agency.
www.RiddickAgency.com

To Mark,

Thank you for being an example of what it means to be a true entrepreneur. Your voice is a gift.

On Purpose,

Table Of Contents

INTRODUCTION
4
Don't Cash That Reality Check **Isha Cogborn**
10
Personal Growth: The Path to Building Your Best Life **Pamela D. Smith**
20
Goal Setting: A Roadmap to Change Your Life **Shawnté Jones**
28
Choosing a Limitless Life **LaToya Jenkins**
42
Unleash the Power of Practice **C. Shaun Owens**
60
Four Keys to Making Your Money Behave **Ericka Young**
70
Preserving Your Legacy: More than Money and Memories
Elaine Cauley
80
Putting an End to People Pleasing **Yubeka Riddick**
88
Living Your Best Life is an Inside Job **Kelli Center**
96
The Cost of Chaos: What Are You Willing to Pay? **La'Vista Jones**
108
How Losing Myself Helped Me Find Myself **Dr. Will Moreland**
120
Is Your Life and Work Slowly Killing You or Is It Feeding Your Soul?
Laurie Battaglia
134
Is the Stress Really Worth It? **Joy Bretz-Sherrill**
144
How to Fire-Proof Your Career **Brenda M. Cunningham**
154
Ask for What Your Desire **Dr. Nadia Brown**
162
Why Social Media Is NOT a Marketing Strategy **Lawrence Riddick**
170
Platform for Purpose: How to Grow Your Audience and Your Impact **Isha Cogborn**
178
CONCLUSION
190

INTRODUCTION

Life is a beautiful gift for you to enjoy. When you discover and walk in your purpose, it becomes a gift to the people who cross your path also.

Living ON PURPOSE provides you with a roadmap that guides the way you spend your time and money, the work you choose, the relationships you cultivate and the way you take care of yourself. This book is fully-packed with sage wisdom and practical advice from collaborators and friends of the **Platform for Purpose Initiative** – an effort I created to amplify the voices of purpose-driven experts and thought leaders.

This is a book that you'll put on the shelf and pull out time and time again as you find yourself experiencing new challenges or being presented with exciting new opportunities. You'll order copies for people you care about and reach out personally to the co-authors who speak to your needs.

Here's what to expect in the next 17 chapters:

I kick things off by focusing on how to avoid discouragement when the people around you don't buy into your dreams. **Pamela D. Smith** will teach you how to develop an intentional mindset and **Shawnté Jones** focuses on how to not only set goals, but she shares some things you can do to actually achieve them. **C. Shaun Owens** demonstrates how the habit of practice can help to create a life of optimal impact.

Are you struggling to find your purpose? **Dr. Will Moreland** poses great questions to take you on a clarity journey, and **Laurie Battaglia** provides a model to assess your alignment between your work and your values.

If you realize your career is no longer a fit and it's time to go, **Joy Bretz-Sherrill** reveals that you don't have to eat beans and rice for the rest of your life to make the transition. She left a career as a corporate treasurer to help stressed-out professionals take back their health and their lives with fitness, nutrition and financial literacy.

Are you in Corporate America? If so, **Brenda Cunningham's** chapter is a must-read. Layoffs have become commonplace in today's economy, but she wants to show you how to become fire-proof in your career so you can keep you neck off the block. **Dr. Nadia Brown's** chapter tells you how to stop leaving money on the table and own your value, whether you're an employee or business owner.

If you're an entrepreneur like me, you know marketing is the lifeblood of business growth. **Lawrence Riddick** lays down tips to create a sustainable marketing strategy that delivers long-term results, not just 'likes' and 'shares'.

I'm a classic overachiever and have unfortunately pushed myself to the point of physical and mental exhaustion more than once. **La'Vista Jones** provides a comprehensive strategy to help business owners avoid burnout by integrating both systems and self-care into your strategy. In **LaToya Jenkins'** chapter, the mother of five and entrepreneur lets us peek behind the curtain to see the important steps she takes to build a happy home while pursuing her passions. I still don't know how she does it!

As much as success is driven by the things we do, it can also be achieved by the things we don't do. **Yubeka Riddick** wants to show you how to overcome people pleasing so you can have

INTRODUCTION

more time and energy to do the work aligned to your purpose.

I was excited when Licensed Professional Counselor **Kelli Center** joined the Platform for Purpose Initiative because we've ignored and stigmatized mental health for far too long – especially in some religious circles where seeking attention for the medical condition is viewed as not having faith in God. Kelli discusses ways to combat anxious and depressed thinking along with strategies to promote emotional wholeness through effective communication in relationships.

If your bank account is creating a barrier between you and your best life, **Ericka Young** will show you how she and her husband paid off $90,000 in debt and how you can make your money behave.

Living your best life can also go beyond your time here on earth. **Elaine Cauley** outlines ways you can leave a legacy for future generations with practical treasures like family recipes and photographs, along with the importance of getting your affairs in order at home and in your business so a long-term illness or death doesn't lead to drama for your loved ones, clients and employees.

I'm excited to be able to curate this project as part of the **Platform for Purpose Initiative**. If your purpose includes connecting to bigger audiences with your message, chapter 17 gives you practical tips to build a platform and personal brand that can expand your impact beyond your wildest dreams.

This book only provides a glimpse of the difference the authors are making in the lives of the people they work with. I encourage you to visit their websites, follow them on social media and access the resources they make available.

Would you like to be featured in the next edition of **On Purpose**? Visit PlatformforPurpose.com to express your interest.

Enjoy!
Isha Cogborn, Editor

LEARN ABOUT
ISHA COGBORN

By Isha Cogborn

Whether she's hosting satellite broadcasts with Oscar-winning actress Hilary Swank, giving career advice in magazines like Ebony and Cosmo, or landing in the top three percent of finalists for a show on the Oprah Winfrey Network, Isha's mission is to help people build the careers of their dreams.

Isha is the founder of Epiphany Institute – a personal development firm that helps people connect their purpose and passion to their profession. She specializes in personal brand building for purpose-driven authors, coaches, consultants and subject-matter experts.

Isha is the host of the podcast, On Purpose with Isha Cogborn and founder of the Platform for Purpose Initiative to amplify the voices of people who want to make a bigger impact in the world. She's the author of personal branding primer, 5 Rules to Win Being You, and the force behind the book, On Purpose: Practical Strategies to Live Your Best Life.

When you work with Isha, it's like hiring three experts in one – a certified life and corporate coach, business strategist and a seasoned PR pro with who served as a global communications and branding manager for one of the world's largest corporations.

Tried by fire, Isha operates with resilience birthed from being a teenage mother on welfare, corporate layoffs, and a bout

Chapter One

of homelessness after a failed business venture. Determined to find purpose in her struggles, Isha founded Startup Life Support in 2017 to help entrepreneurs overcome the fear, frustration and isolation of starting a business.

Isha earned a degree in Broadcast and Cinematic Arts from Central Michigan University. She's a member of Alpha Kappa Alpha Sorority, Inc. and a volunteer with Kauffman Foundation's 1 Million Cups initiative.

Connect with Isha Cogborn

Website: EpiphanyInstitute.com
Podcast: OnPurposePodcast.com
Facebook: @coachisha
LinkedIn: Isha Cogborn
Email: Isha@EpiphanyInstitute.com

Don't Cash That Reality Check!

ISHA COGBORN

Think back to your earliest childhood memories. What did you want to be when you grew up? A doctor? Astronaut? Superman?

No matter how ambitious or exotic your aspirations were, the grown-ups in your life likely affirmed you. But at some point, they felt compelled to let you know what you were shooting for was unrealistic.

The five-footer is told to hang up his hoop dreams. The teenage girl is told that she'll never excel in that male-dominated field, so she might as well save herself the frustration. People call the middle-aged engineer crazy for walking away from a secure job and stable salary to pursue his life-long dream of starting a business.

But who gets to decide what's realistic or not?

OVERDRAFT CHARGES AND THE END OF YOUR DREAMS

In 2017, banks and credit unions in the United States collected $34.3 billion in overdraft fees, according to Moebs Services. Consumer watchdog groups point out that those who are disproportionately affected by the charges are the most financially vulnerable.

The journey to pursue the career of your dreams is a lot like

Chapter One

maintaining a checking account. We all know that the most important thing to remember when you have a checking account is to keep more money in it than you spend. When good things happen, whether you find an investor for your business, get an opportunity you don't think you are qualified for or land a new client, your account balance grows. Every time you face a negative occurrence – you don't get the promotion or you seem to run into another brick wall – your balance shrinks.

With more than a decade spent coaching entrepreneurs and corporate professionals, I've found that just like financially vulnerable folks are hit the hardest by overdraft fees, emotional vulnerabilities planted early in life can make every disappointment sting even harder.

Don't Cash That Reality Check!

Withdrawals also come in the form of reality checks. A reality check is when some well-meaning (or not-so-well-meaning) person tries to get you to recognize that what you're pursuing isn't a good idea.

Reality checks come in a variety of shapes and sizes. Here are a few you may encounter frequently:

Historical Reality Check

Based on your past, the person issuing the reality check can't see how what you are pursuing is possible for you.

My freshman year of high school was horrible. I was the victim of mean girl drama, often skipping class to avoid the taunts of the opposing tribe. What happens when you don't go to class? *Your grades reflect it.*

Fast forward to the beginning of my junior year: I made an appointment to see my counselor, Mr. Kramer, to change my schedule. I had signed up for an office skills class but decided to take small business management instead.

CHAPTER ONE

Mr. Kramer pulled out my file, looked at my grades from freshman year and said, "You need to keep this class so that you can get an entry-level clerical job when you graduate."

"I have an entry-level clerical job now. I'm going to college when I graduate," I replied strongly.

"You're not going to college with grades like these," he said.

After several rounds of battle, he finally agreed to change my class. I also demanded a change in counselors.

Was Mr. Kramer a terrible person? I don't think so. A terrible counselor maybe, but not a terrible person. In fact, he probably thought he was doing me a favor by trying to keep me from getting my hopes up about going to college when my grades were less than stellar.

He found it necessary to write me a reality check to convince me to downsize my ambitions, but I didn't cash that reality check. I worked even harder, went to college, and graduated with a higher grade-point average than I had in high school.

Over the years, I found out that Mr. Kramer told a lot of students in my high school that they wouldn't make it to college. And sadly, a lot of them believed him. I have made it my personal mission to undo the damage of the Mr. Kramers of the world who keep people from going after what they really want.

Far too many people count themselves out before they even try simply because someone told them it wasn't possible. My goal is to teach you to move beyond the voices of pessimism so that you can focus on the career and life that you really want.

No matter how many times you've blown it in the past, success is still within your grasp. Yes, there may be consequences for your previous actions (or inactions), but that doesn't mean you're forever doomed.

Isha Cogborn

Mirrored Reality Check

Another type of reality check is when the issuers base their expectations of you on their expectations of themselves. Think about it: Parents who are college graduates automatically expect that their children will be college graduates as well. And unfortunately, if parents have low expectations of themselves, they may also have low expectations of their children.

This can happen with employers, colleagues, business partners, and of course, family members. I gave birth to my son, Deon, during my freshman year of college. Since the day I found out I was expecting, it was my plan to return to campus with my son and maintain a full-time schedule. The school was over two hours away from my family and my mother didn't think it was a good idea to be so far away from home with a small child. She tried to convince me to either go to school closer to home or allow her to raise Deon until I graduated. Neither of these were attractive options to me.

Did my mother lack confidence in my ability to be a mom and a college student? I don't even think she gave it a thought. But what she did think about was how challenging it was for her as a single mother with three young children. She thought of the hardships she faced on a daily basis, and she didn't want her baby girl to struggle that way.

If someone doesn't buy into your dream, it's not necessarily a lack of faith in you personally. But if they can't picture themselves being able to do it, they may not be able to picture you successfully doing it either.

Statistical Reality Checks

You want to start a business. They tell you that half of all businesses fail in the first five years.

You want to run for office. They tell you that 90% of elected officials are white.

You have your sights set on running the company one day.

CHAPTER ONE

They tell you that only 6.6% of Fortune 500 CEOs are women.

As Mark Twain said, "There are three types of lies: Lies, damned lies and statistics." Statistics are not always facts. They are often numbers that can be easily manipulated to support whatever viewpoint the sharer wants to drive home. They can be taken out of context, and people rarely tell the story behind the numbers.

Even if the stats paint a bleak picture of your odds of success, remember that people beat the odds every day.

Why not you?

ISSUE A STOP PAYMENT ON REALITY CHECKS

Please don't walk away from this chapter thinking I'm telling you not to consider the opinions of others. Sound counsel is absolutely critical to career and business success. However, you cannot afford to blindly accept every piece of advice thrown your way. Perhaps what they're telling you is true. But maybe it isn't. Also remember that what's true for others doesn't mean it will be true for you.

You can't make decisions about your future based on flippant comments or opinions. You owe it to yourself to do your research, which may lead you to a course of action that will bring success for you, even if it has been elusive to others. While your dream is in the incubation stage, recognize that you may not be able to share it with everyone. Some people just won't get it. Until you've built up enough confidence in your ability to move forward, you may wish to limit your communication to just a trusted, positive few.

KEEP YOUR ACCOUNT POSITIVE

We can't avoid what people say and no matter how hard we try, unsupportive comments can shake our confidence. Here are three tips to make sure that you keep your balance positive:

Isha Cogborn

Tip #1: Avoid negative people, places and things.

This may be a hard pill to swallow, but the most negative person in your life could be you. We all have voices in our heads. What are yours saying? Are the messages loving and affirming or are they harsh and critical? Others may have contributed to the programming, but only you have the power to change it.

Take a look at your routine behaviors. Are they getting you closer to the life you want or are you sabotaging yourself? From food to media and entertainment, we are products of what we consume. Have you noticed that conversations with certain people leave you feeling depleted? Does watching the news leave you anxious or fearful?

While you can't live in a bubble and still make a difference in the world, you can be very deliberate about who and what you allow in your space. Keep conversations with complaining co-workers and family members to a minimum. If social media is a trigger, use it sparingly.

Tip #2: Make deposits into yourself daily.

Daily deposits are about reminding yourself who you are and what you want. It's a way to reprogram the voices in your head and uproot unproductive habits. Daily deposits help to keep us focused on our purpose and help to undo the damage that comes from living in a negative world.

Here are a few tactics to consider:

- Meditation and prayer
- Affirmations
- Creating a vision board and reviewing it daily
- Reviewing your goals every morning
- Creating a playlist of music that inspires you.

Tip #3: Surround Yourself with Rich People

Do I mean people with a lot of money? Maybe, but not necessarily. When I talk about rich people, I'm talking about people who make you better.

Every successful person needs three people in their lives: a mentor, a cheerleader and a challenger.

You need a mentor to show you the ropes. A mentor is someone who is wise and knowledgeable and can shorten your learning curve.

A cheerleader is someone who believes in you unconditionally. No matter how inconceivable your dream may appear to be, your cheerleader is going to be behind you 110%.

And finally, you need a challenger. A challenger will ask you the tough questions, and it's okay if you don't always know the answers immediately. A trusted external perspective can help you avoid struggles by proactively identifying issues you don't see.

HOW'S YOUR ACCOUNT?

Someone said that most people die between the ages of 22-30; they just delay the funeral. Here's the bottom line: When you stop dreaming, you start dying. And there are plenty of people who should be charged as accomplices in the murder of your aspirations.

While there are certainly people who just don't want to see you succeed, most of the dream crushers in your life actually have your best interest at heart. However, they think the odds are stacked against you, and they simply don't want to see you go through the pain of failure.

Don't set your aspirations based on the support of the people around you. Set them *On Purpose*. Trailblazers have to be willing to chart a course that others simply may not understand.

Keep going…they'll see it once you succeed.

Isha Cogborn

YOUR ASSIGNMENT

Carefully and truthfully answer the following questions:

1. What reasons have people given you about why your plans may not work?
2. On a scale of 0 to 5, with 0 being 'not at all' and 5 being 'I absolutely believe it', how are the objections of others affecting your confidence in your ability to succeed?
3. If you rated anything above 0, what evidence do you have that these things are absolutely true for you?
4. What will it take to bring your belief down to a zero for the objections affecting your confidence?
5. Who can you recruit as your mentor, cheerleader and challenger?

To hear inspirational stories of ordinary people who are bold enough to pursue their dreams, subscribe to my podcast at **OnPurposePodcast.com.**

LEARN ABOUT
Pamela
D. Smith

Pamela D. Smith is a certified life coach who empowers women to grow into their next desired level. She knows what it's like to feel stuck and wants to help you go from enduring life to enjoying life.

A certified coach with the John Maxwell Team, Pam is also an award-winning performer and trainer in the airline industry. She is passionate about personal growth and with her support, clients are experiencing results in months that others take years to accomplish on their own.

With a life-long passion of encouraging and helping others, Pam is an avid volunteer supporting both domestic and international causes, including serving as a small group leader focused on personal growth at Faith Christian Center, in Phoenix, Arizona.

In her free time, she enjoys traveling and spending time with the loves of her life: Her husband, children and grandchildren.

Connect with Pam

Website: Pamhasfavor.com
Facebook: @pamhasfavor
Email: Pam@Pamhasfavor.com

Chapter Two

Personal Growth: The Path to Building Your Best Life

PAMELA D. SMITH

Can you imagine living your life to its fullest potential? Doing something that you've always wanted to do and loving every aspect of it?

Twenty-five years ago, I felt stuck on a treadmill going nowhere. I was living life day in and day out with no passion or purpose. That's when I started my personal growth journey.

Personal growth is one of the few things you can't buy with money; it requires intention, effort and commitment. However, the return on investment can payout beyond your wildest dreams.

When I became intentional about my personal growth, I was able to uncover talents that I didn't know existed. I began to see what was possible for me, but I needed to be consistent if I wanted my potential to become my reality.

As I saw the life that I wanted taking shape, one of my greatest desires became helping others reach their full potential, too. But I quickly learned that I can't make anyone grow. I can only plant or water the seeds.

Personal growth is essential to your health, your happiness, your finances and your spiritual and emotional wellness, but it doesn't automatically come with age like gray hairs or wrinkled skin. It's a choice. When we make the choice, we put ourselves on the course to go from simply enduring life to enjoying life.

Chapter Two

> *"Personal growth doesn't come with age like gray hairs or wrinkled skin; it's a choice."*

CONSTRUCTING YOUR BEST LIFE

You have the power to build the life of your dreams! Building your best life is much like building your dream home. When you have the tools you need and take the necessary steps, you'll build a strong, beautiful life that produces endless opportunities.

THE BLUEPRINT: YOUR ACTION PLAN

Could you imagine yourself paying a huge down payment on your dream home with no one ever showing you a photo of what they were building? That's how many of us live our lives. We never get a picture of what we want, so we set goals haphazardly and struggle to achieve them.

Think about an area of your life where you'd like to see improvement. What is your goal? Now, think about what it will take to get there. What will you need to do and how often? What do you need to STOP doing? What is a reasonable timeline to achieve it?

Just like you wouldn't expect your contractor to build your dream home in a day, you can't lose 100 pounds or get out of a considerable amount of debt overnight, either. Your goals can be aggressive, but they should not be self-defeating.

LAYING THE FOUNDATION WITH AN INTENTIONAL MINDSET

When you set out to make positive changes in your life, you're likely to meet resistance. Instead of focusing on the challenges, I encourage you to build your best life on the foundation of an intentional mindset.

Oxford Living Dictionary defines intentional as, "done

CHAPTER TWO

on purpose; deliberate." An intentional mindset leads to thoughtful choices, which move us closer to achieving our goals. Don't be surprised if it's not easy, though. Here are four of the common barriers to an intentional mindset and ways to overcome them:

Assumption Barrier

What things do you expect to be true, even though you have no evidence? Are these assumptions leading you to take the wrong actions or no actions at all? One of the assumptions that I made early in my professional life was that advancement would just naturally occur. I later realized it required intentional planning and actions to position myself for the opportunities I desired.

Are you assuming you can't achieve the results you desire because of your age, ethnicity, education level, gender, geographic location or socio-economic status? What evidence do you have to support your assumptions? For every reason (or excuse) you give for why it's not possible, there's another reason that says that it is possible.

Perfection Barrier

Personal growth is about progression, not perfection. Don't expect yourself to master every new thing you attempt. Instead, be willing to try new things, embrace learning opportunities and celebrate incremental improvements.

Comparison Barrier

Social media makes it easy to look at other people's lives and accomplishments and feel like you're coming up short. Truth is, we never know the full story of anyone's life but our own. We don't know how hard they've worked, what challenges they've endured or if they're even happy!

There's no one else just like you. Instead of comparing yourself to someone else, stay focused on your unique journey and the life you're working to create.

Fear Barrier

Fear is a natural emotion, but it's not always rational. Instead of expecting the absence of fear, find ways to work through it. Preparation is a valuable tool you can use to fight fear.

When I started my coaching practice, I committed to hosting a weekly livestream to discuss personal growth topics. To say I was nervous is an understatement...and it showed. But instead of assuming people wouldn't benefit from what I had to say or expecting myself to deliver perfectly on-air when I hadn't done it before, I resisted the urge to compare myself to more poised speakers and pushed through the fear. These broadcasts are a part of my own personal growth journey, and I get to help others in the process!

Although these barriers may be a factor in your journey, they don't have to hinder your ability to grow. Challenge yourself every day to function with an intentional mindset. Here's what it looks like in your day-to-day life:

Accidental Mindset	Intentional Mindset
I'll start later	I'll start right now
Growth will come automatically	I take responsibility for my growth
Falls into bad habits	Fights for good habits
Plays it safe	Gets out of the comfort zone
Applies minimal effort	Applies full potential
Stops learning after graduation	Never stops learning

CHAPTER TWO

THE WALLS OF SELF-AWARENESS

Walls are a critical element to the structure of a home because they protect you from the elements of the outside world. Could you imagine living in a home with no walls? When you don't understand yourself, you're more vulnerable to the harsh elements of everyday life – criticism, accusations, unmet expectations, and the list goes on.

Why is self-awareness so important? When you understand yourself and have a clear perception of your personality, strengths, weaknesses, likes and dislikes, you're empowered to make the necessary adjustments as you continue to grow. It takes sincerity, too; not being unduly harsh with yourself or making excuses in areas that need attention.

How Do You Develop Self-Awareness?

Make a list of your strengths and your weaknesses. Ask family, friends and colleagues what they see as your strengths and weaknesses (you may want to do this in writing). What are the common themes that emerge? Are there strengths they see that you never recognized in yourself? Your co-workers or professional contacts may have a very different perspective of you than your friends and family.

Keeping a journal can also be a wonderful tool to clear your thoughts, get to know yourself better and document your personal growth journey.

Set aside time daily to think about yourself: Your goals, how you're executing against your plans, and any barriers or mindset issues that are hindering you. What people, places or things energize you? What or who drains your energy?

Practicing self-awareness allows you to focus on the things you can control instead of feeling powerless to the circumstances around you.

Pamela D. Smith

A POSITIVE ATTITUDE: THE SKY IS THE LIMIT!

Just like the walls, a roof protects inhabitants of a home from the outside elements. A positive attitude can function as your protection from being dragged down and discouraged by situations beyond your control.

Although you may not be able to change your situation or circumstances immediately, you can instantly change your attitude. You have the power to choose a positive attitude even in negative situations. Your attitude will determine how you view every situation. It will determine your reaction, and it even has the ability to influence the outcome.

AN ATTITUDE OF GRATITUDE

Gratitude can put a new perspective on every area of your life and open doors for you to achieve all you desire. When you count your blessings, you take your focus off of what's wrong and appreciate what's right.

5 Practical Steps to Develop a Positive Attitude

1. Instead of focusing on the problem, think about what will empower you to successfully move forward.
2. Read quotes and/or affirmations that align with the attitude you want to reflect.
3. Spend time every day in prayer and meditation.
4. Listen to your inner voice and take notice when it shifts to a negative tone.
5. Use positive vocabulary. Here are a few examples:

Negative Vocabulary	Positive Vocabulary
I have to go to work.	I get to go to work. I'm grateful to have a job!
I have to take the kids to school.	I'm blessed to have children, and I get to take them to school.
I must exercise.	I have the ability to exercise. I'm going to do it!
Gas is so expensive.	I'm grateful to have a car to put gas in.
I hate cleaning the house.	It's wonderful to have a house to clean.

CHAPTER TWO

Personal growth requires action. No one can make you grow; it's an inside job. But once you commit to growth, you'll find the outside world aligning with the people, resources and opportunities you need to create the life you desire.

The people in your life may not understand your desire to change, and that's okay. Whether it's a drastic lifestyle change or just picking up a new hobby, you don't have to justify your decisions to the people around you.

Be willing to try new things, embrace imperfection and push through fear. Things won't always go the way you want them to and you'll likely experience challenges along the way. You are not a failure – even when you fail. Challenges will make you more resilient and appreciative of the results you achieve.

Don't be so anxious to accomplish your goals that you miss the lessons along the way. Each journey will prepare you for the next. To learn how I can help you reach your next desired level, email me at *pam@pamhasfavor.com*.

Let's go and grow!

Pamela D. Smith

27

LEARN ABOUT
SHAWNTÉ JONES
PHR, SHRM-CP

Shawnté Jones is a human resource professional, adjunct professor and coach who helps early-stage professionals break through barriers to achieve their personal definition of success.

By day, Shawnté works directly with leaders and hiring managers in a major corporation, helping them locate and develop the right talent as part of the human resources staff. She has a unique understanding of the challenges faced by employees who struggle to fit in, meaningfully connect or who lack the boldness to speak up and share their brilliance.

Her passion for professional development and desire to see all people succeed led her to launch Be Bold Enterprises, where she helps young professionals close the gap between them and the opportunities they desire. Shawnté's first book, *I Have Talents, And I am Not Afraid* to Use Them helps readers overcome fear, complacency, negative behavior and outside influences to reap the rewards of a more purposeful life.

Shawnté earned a B.S. in Communication from University of Houston-Clear Lake and an M.S. in Human Resource Development from University of Houston.

Connect with Shawnté
Email: Shawnte@TheBeBoldEnterprises.com
Website:@BeBoldEnterprises
LinkedIn: Shawnté Jones

Chapter Three

Goal Setting: A Roadmap to Change Your Life

SHAWNTÉ JONES PHR, SHRM-CP

What do you want to achieve in your life? What expectations do you have for yourself, both short and long-term? Far too many people live their lives without a sense of real direction. They're simply going through the motions and accepting what comes their way.

What if you had a system to help you achieve more than you ever thought possible? The answer isn't complicated or expensive, and it's probably something you're already familiar with. Want to know the answer?

Goal setting.

You may be required to create goals at work, as many companies use this as a way to manage performance. But do you follow the same practice for the things that are important to you personally?

Having a goal or aspiration in your head isn't enough. Documenting what you want establishes a level of accountability. It helps you to prioritize what's most important so that you can channel your energy and resources accordingly. Even if changing circumstances facilitate a need to adjust your plans or approach to reaching the goal, the odds of moving beyond obstacles to achieve it will be much greater.

Documenting your aspirations is a way of proclaiming that

Chapter Three

what you want is truly important because you are intentionally setting it apart from the thousands of other thoughts that enter and exit your mind each day. Having documented goals, regardless of your background, sets you apart and provides you with metrics to determine your personal effectiveness.

As you achieve your goals, it fuels momentum that will push you to achieving even greater accomplishments than what you initially set out to do.

You probably have an idea of what you want to achieve. You may want to get a better paying job, get out of debt, get married, to buy a house in the suburbs or become an entrepreneur. These are all notable accomplishments, but how do you transform your daydreams, fantasies and imagination into reality? What actions do you need to take? Goal setting elevates you from wanting to achieving.

LONGING FOR MORE

When I reflect back on my adult life, I started out "going with the flow". After my planned degree choice was eliminated, I pursued the path that the college established as an alternative. I wasn't passionate about becoming an administrative specialist, but I made the most out of the opportunities presented and became more intentional about what I did want. I studied the high achievers at work and picked up on a key life lesson— setting personal goals.

Setting life goals wasn't a part of the conversation in my house when I was growing up. The focus was to go to work, collect the paycheck and make sure the financial responsibilities were taken care of. Even as a child, I knew I wanted more than that, but it took years into adulthood before the desires of my heart were accompanied with plans. Through observation, I realized that a purpose-driven life involves creating strategic goals, putting action plans in place, and actually doing what you say you're going to do.

CHAPTER THREE

BENEFITS OF PERSONAL GOAL SETTING

When it comes to goal setting, January is overrated. Crafting a goal in September is just as good as setting the goal in January as long as the timing aligns with your ability to accomplish it. Don't feel like you have to hold off until the new year to take action.

From earning multiple degrees and publishing my first book to achieving financial milestones and starting my professional development business, my experiences have revealed the following benefits of personal goal setting:

Goals Provide Focus

Establishing goals forces you to focus your efforts and energy. If you simply have aspirations floating around in your head, you're almost guaranteed to get overwhelmed by everything else going on in your life. When distractions come, your aspirations move to the back burner. No matter how efficient you are, there are still only 24 hours in a day. To achieve your goals, you'll most likely have to say "no" to a few less important activities.

Goals Keep You Motivated

Goals that are written down will serve as a motivator and a tool to hold you accountable. When you can visualize yourself in a positive future state, it will compel you to move forward. Tracking the progress of your goals will push you towards achievement. If you love to check the boxes on your to-do list, you'll find it hard not to keep the commitment.

Goals Build Confidence

Once you develop a track record of achieving your goals, your level of confidence will soar through the roof. You are proving to yourself and others that you have the ability to keep your commitments. Before you know it, you'll be setting even bigger goals.

In 2016, I published my first book, "I Have Talents, And I am Not Afraid to Use Them." Just like you, I had a million other things on my plate, and there were times that I felt like giving up. By refocusing on why it was important to finish the book - which was to help others, I mustered the discipline to get the project across the finish line.

Becoming a published author and receiving positive feedback from readers created a level of confidence in me that I would not have experienced otherwise. There's a euphoria that comes from achieving your goals that exceeds the efforts invested - if you're pursuing the right goals.

YOUR ROADMAP FOR SETTING PERSONAL GOALS

The act of simply writing your goals down will make you more effective than keeping your aspirations in your head. Following this six-step process will increase the chances of you not only achieving your goals, but you'll also be able to work on the right things and work around the challenges that life may send your way.

Use the following steps to develop your customized strategy to creating your best life.

Step 1: Visioning

The process starts with taking a step back to look at the big picture. Let's say you want to save more money. Why do you want to save more money? If you simply set a goal to save more money, that could be as little as $1 a week. At the end of the year, you will have saved $52. But if you're trying to save for a down payment on a house with such a vague goal, plan on moving in around the year 2404! Having a clear vision of what you ultimately want to achieve will help you set the right goals.

As you are working towards creating your vision, you may find it helpful to create a vision board to keep the picture of what you are working towards in front of you. You can find a workshop on creating vision boards or you can create one on your own.

CHAPTER THREE

Step 2: Brainstorming

There's likely more than one approach to achieving your vision. Brainstorming allows you to think through multiple paths that could lead you there so you can create the plan that's best for you.

Look at each major element from your vision and think of all of the ways you can achieve it. Start by listing all of your ideas in short form. It is important to write out whatever comes to mind; don't judge your ideas at this stage in the exercise.

A recommendation for this exercise is to create a cluster list with each major part of the vision written out in the middle of the page, and write all the ideas related to achieving this part of your vision using the clusters around that major part. For example, if a major part of your vision is to achieve wealth, place achieving wealth in the middle of the page and then write out all the ideas on how to achieve wealth. Sample ideas to achieve wealth are: Purchase a home, invest in real estate, freelance, increase 401k contribution, etc.

Purchase a home
Invest in Real Estate
(Wealth)
Increase 401K Contribution
Freelance

Continue to list out ideas until you have exhausted them for this subject. Once you finish, move on to the next subject. The beauty of brainstorming is that there are no wrong answers, and you may come back to some of these ideas later even if you decide they're not a part of your immediate plans.

Step 3: Planning

In the planning step of the process, you'll review all of the possibilities and determine the actions you will take to make achieving your vision possible. This involves reviewing your resources and breaking it down into the who, what, when, where, and how.

Ask yourself questions relevant to your strategic goal such as the following:

- What do you already have access to?
- How can you use what you already have?
- How can someone help you?
- Who can help you?
- What educational resources are available to elevate your knowledge?
- What do you need to start doing?
- What do you need to stop doing?
- What are the milestones to chart your progress?
- Where might you run into obstacles or setbacks?

Once you've analyzed the possibilities, chosen your best course of action and thought through the resources you have, the resources you need, and potential challenges, use the information you've gathered to write a general plan or deliverables. Do this for each element of your vision.

Depending on the complexity of your vision, this may look different from person to person or plan to plan. The important thing is that it provides enough detail to give you a clear picture of what you want to accomplish. This will prepare you for the next step of defining the measurable goals.

Keep in mind that all of the planning in the world won't guarantee success, but it will help you proactively

CHAPTER THREE

address potential problems and utilize your resources effectively. During the planning phase, you can also enlist someone like me to consult with to make sure you are not missing critical elements in your strategy.

Step 4: Documenting

Documenting is perhaps the most critical step in the process. A study* conducted by Dr. Gail Matthews and Dominican University showed that when people wrote down their goals, they were 44% more successful in achieving them than those who kept their desires in their heads.

One of the most widely used methods for documenting goals is to use the SMART technique. This acronym means Specific, Measurable, Attainable, Relevant and Time-bound. When you write out your goals, use the five elements from the SMART acronym to make a complete strategy statement.

For example, your goal is to save enough money for a down payment on a house. To write this as a SMART strategy, you can formulate it as, "In order to have a 20% down payment on a $200,000 house without having to borrow money, I will save $13,400 each year for the next three years."

This statement makes it clear what you want to do, how you will do it and the duration of time it will take to make it happen. When writing your strategies, you must be clear about what you want. This is why the pre-work of visioning, brainstorming and planning are important. Document all of your strategies in the same manner.

Step 5: Implementing

Your strategies must be actionable, which means that they can be implemented by you or through your resources. You can have stretch goals, but if your strategies can not be attainable within a reasonable

---

*"STUDY DEMONSTRATES THAT WRITING GOALS ENHANCES GOAL ACHIEVEMENT." Dominican University of California, 5 Jan. 22017, www.dominican.edu/dominicannews/study-demonstrates-that-writing-goals-enhances-goal-achievement.

amount of time, you run the risk of becoming discouraged.

Before beginning the implementation process, set targets for when you anticipate hitting each milestone. Think of them as mile markers when running a race. Be sure to keep your strategies easily accessible for you to view. When you see your strategies written out, you are more likely to continue working towards them. Having the printed version of your goals in a prominent location will allow you to review them regularly, to track your progress and to stay honest with yourself about what you have committed to do.

You may also want to recruit an accountability partner to check in with on a regular basis. The Dominican University Study also found that those who sent a weekly update to a friend about their goals were 70% more likely to accomplish them than those who kept their written goals to themselves.

Step 6: Evaluating

It is critical to evaluate your progress to make sure that what you are doing continues to align with SMART strategies and the overall vision. Ask yourself, "If I continue the same effort going forward, how likely am I to achieve my goal or vision?"

If you experienced any pitfalls, setbacks or even unexpected successes, you'll want to evaluate the impact it could make on your initial strategy and timeline. Be willing to make adjustments if you are not progressing on schedule or if changes to your circumstances no longer allow you to follow your original course of action.

Also evaluate whether your resources are producing what you expected. For example, if you took on a part-time retail job as part of your savings strategy but you spend all of your earnings in the store, you may need to

CHAPTER THREE

rethink your approach. Schedule check-ins with yourself throughout the process and again at the conclusion of the timeframe set to achieve your goal – whether you accomplished it as expected or not. Evaluating your efforts will give you valuable insight about yourself and will help you to be more successful in the future.

Do you want to change your life for the better? Start by documenting your vision and personal strategy to achieve it. You have the power to turn your dreams into reality. By following this six-step approach to developing your personal strategy, you will create a habit of focusing on what's important. You will gain confidence, your performance will improve and you will be motivated to continue to do great things.

A STRATEGY TO LIVE YOUR BEST LIFE
I began incorporating a yearly vision board into my goal-writing process. As I look back on my accomplishments like writing a book and even being able to cross several fun things off of my bucket list, I can clearly see how much of an impact having a strategic plan for my life played in those achievements.

While it is time consuming to start and maintain the process, having a vision and documenting goals to achieve it has created opportunities for me that I didn't even know were possible. I'd rather invest the time to document what I want than to live with the frustration of knowing I could have and be so much more.

Here's an important truth: You won't always accomplish every goal you set out to achieve. However, do not be afraid to set goals simply because you don't want to fail. The act of documenting your goals and working to achieve them will instill a routine and habits that will lead to a more effective life.

Be willing to start small if necessary in order to generate a track record of success. Also make it a practice to revisit your goals to make sure they align with your vision.

Shawnté Jones

If you are willing to invest the right level of time and commitment into achieving your goals and keep your eyes focused on the vision, you'll find yourself standing in the middle of a purpose-filled life that you love. For tips and strategies to help you achieve your personal goals, connect with me (Shawnte' Jones) on LinkedIn.

LEARN ABOUT
LaToya JENKINS

LaToya Jenkins is an author and productivity consultant for women and families. A devoted wife and dedicated mother of five children, LaToya and her husband own three businesses: Jenkins Law Firm, where she serves as the business operations manager, A Themed Event, and Buy Now Properties.

LaToya is passionate about serving families and her community and hosts annual community-building events. She is a committee member of the Brain Injury Alliance of Arizona, a regional board member of YoungLife Arizona, and a developmental board member of Elevate Phoenix. LaToya also enjoys traveling and competing in marathons and triathlons.

How does she do it all with a husband and five children? That's what everyone always wants to know. After having her second child, she discovered tons of challenges in trying to balance family, business, and community. She began researching and developing practical strategies to overcome those challenges and live a full and uncompromising life. In 2013, she began mentoring other women and families with those strategies. Today, she has touched over 100 families as she continues to walk out her dreams.

Chapter Four

A rare native of Las Vegas, Nevada, LaToya now resides in Mesa, Arizona with her family.

Connect with LaToya Jenkins:
Email: info@latoyajenkins.com
Website: www.latoyajenkins.com
Facebook: @latoyajenkins.limitlessliving
Phone: 480-530-0660

Choosing a Limitless Life

LaToya Jenkins

This summer, our family of seven took a trip to Cancun, Mexico. It was the first time my husband and I traveled internationally with all five kids, and it was quite an adventure. The kids had been looking forward to going to the beach for months, and we had a ton of outdoor activities planned, including tours, watersport activities, golfing, and lazy days by the pool. The kids were expecting a grand vacation, and so were we.

When we landed in Cancun, it was raining. At first, we barely noticed the rain as we snapped pictures outside of the airport while waiting for our hotel shuttle. But soon after the selfies were done, the sprinkles turned into drops, and the drops turned into a full-out downpouring. We were running for cover and were drenched by the time we made it into the freezing-cold shuttle. Everyone was shivering, but we were still smiling and eager to get our vacation started.

It poured for four of the seven days we were there. Our outdoor activities were literally a wash, and we spent most of our time searching for a break in the clouds. Let me tell you that keeping five energetic kids happy in a hotel for five days when they were expecting to be on the beach was no easy feat! Despite the rain, we were determined to have a good time. We turned every buffet trip into an adventure, explored every indoor activity possible at the hotel and even squeezed in some pool time during a couple of breaks in the clouds. We got caught in the rain several times and had to employ some

Chapter Four

serious ingenuity to redirect meltdowns and create fun in what could have been a stressful situation. By Day 6, the clouds were gone and the sun was shining brilliantly.

When we returned to Phoenix, it took some time to retrieve all of our luggage from baggage claim for our family of seven. While we waited, a woman approached me and asked if all the kids with me were mine. I laughed, and we struck up a conversation. She and a friend were staying at our hotel and were watching us the entire time. Some of what they witnessed was pure comedy, but most importantly, they saw us living our best lives. We were in the midst of chaos and unexpected circumstances after we had planned the perfect vacation, and yet we were working it out with joy and smiles on our faces. As it turns out, she was an editor for a magazine and asked me to write for a parenting column.

Many of our friends and family were perplexed by the fact that we would even have the audacity to believe we'd enjoy a trip with our crew of high needs kids. But we've had far too many amazing experiences by choosing to live a limitless life. We encounter many of the same challenges that any other family deals with, but choosing a limitless life is what drives us to face those challenges head on - even enjoying ourselves in the process. Rain comes, and when it does, we choose to dance in it.

CAN YOU REALLY HAVE IT ALL?

Women are uniquely equipped to dance in the rain. Most of us have heard the story of Eve being formed from the rib of Adam. The ribs have two important functions. They expand and contract to allow movement, and they protect the vital organs. Wives and mothers - as the ribs - are uniquely equipped to adjust and maneuver when necessary. We are uniquely equipped to protect the things that we love and are important. And we do it with grace.

But it's not always easy. Over the last 20 years, technological advancements have accelerated at a greater rate than at any other period in history. We have become a global village.

CHAPTER FOUR

Information, tips and tools for raising up families are available at our fingertips, and at the same time, women are being given more and better opportunities in the workplace and greater influence in their communities. Many of us see the possibilities of having it all. We believe that we can have a thriving family and a dynamic life outside of the home, but sometimes it's hard to connect the dots. We may want to have it all and believe that it is possible, but we still find it difficult to apply that desire and belief to our day-to-day lives. I've spent the last 14 years discovering, applying and sharing those practical ways to live a limitless life even in the midst of responsibilities, and yes, sometimes chaos.

Since giving birth to my first child, I've been a work from home mom, a stay at home mom, a work away from home mom and every other combination in between. I have five children, and my husband LaShawn and I own three businesses. By the time we had our second child, I wanted to stay home with my babies to nourish them and to be there for every milestone. But I also wanted to share my gifts and talents with the world beyond the four walls of my home and make good on a promise my husband and I made to one another. Shortly after we married, we promised that we wouldn't lose sight of ourselves while doing this family thing. We both saw that our life purposes were bigger than our family, and we wanted to make room to fulfill those purposes.

However, having a great commission in your heart and actually accomplishing it are two different things. Trying to juggle everything with grace wasn't easy, and I came across many challenges over the next several years. We had more babies, started businesses and were actively volunteering three times a week at our church. We were serving on boards in our community, traveling, volunteering, and engaging in several extra-curricular activities as a family. We were committed to living a limitless life, but after a while, the life I enjoyed so much made me feel overwhelmed, overextended, and a bunch of other "overs".

Daily, I faced challenges with feeling guilty over neglecting something or someone, facing self-care deficiencies, and not

LaToya Jenkins

fully balancing time and energy between work and newborns and toddlers. I was trying with everything in me to be someone my family actually enjoyed being around instead of being a crabby and contentious complainer.

I often wondered if I was trying to do too much. I remember sitting down one day to plan out my week, and I felt pure dread. I had a lot on my plate and didn't know how I would keep it together. I knew something had to change. I decided it was time to become more intentional in the details of my life if I was going to live it abundantly. I evaluated every angle and researched practical ways to improve the quality of my life and bring my joy back. The truth is there was no magic wand I could wave to make everything fall into place, but discovering how to be proactive in achieving the vision for my life rather than just letting life happen to me gave me more grace to get it together.

I spent several years developing strategies that have unleashed grace in my life and effectively bought me peace, sanity and the belief that I really could achieve my best life. I began helping other women with the same practical strategies and I am confident that they will work for you as well. We all want to live our best lives. We have dreams and visions that our hearts are burning to carry out. But often, the realities of our day to day lives make those dreams feel afar off. We need grace to make it all work for us.

THREE KEYS TO A LIMITLESS LIFE

I have often been asked how I manage to juggle my roles without dropping the balls all over the place. The answer is grace. And I've discovered that there are three key areas where grace can be practically activated. They are energy, time and support.

Energy
en·er·gy - the strength and vitality required for sustained physical or mental activity.

How much do you have in your tank? Is it enough to sustain

CHAPTER FOUR

you? What are you putting in and how much is coming out? Are you running on fumes or is your tank overflowing? You can have all the best intentions in the world and schedule your time in such a way that you squeeze something out of every minute of the day, but if you don't have the energy to do what is demanded of you, your intentions will be unrealized. Your time will be wasted.

We've all been there before. You were working up against a project deadline with little sleep, and you hit a wall when your mental energy fizzled out. You planned to spend the afternoon playing with your kids, but you ended up putting them in front of the television because you were physically drained and could do little more than sit on the couch. Or perhaps there was a time when the demands of work and the demands of home were at odds, causing you to feel emotionally drained. At some point we've all experienced a lack of energy. Likewise, many of us have heard the phrase "secure your own oxygen mask first before helping others." Think about it. If an airplane cabin was to lose oxygen and you tried to secure someone else's oxygen mask before securing your own, you might pass out trying to help them and possibly not even get their mask secured. By evaluating your own energy needs and proactively planning to meet them, you will be tapping into an important area of grace that will allow you to finish your race and help others.

KAT'S STORY
Kat is a lawyer friend of mine who gave birth to twins a few years ago. She and her husband struggled with infertility for years and had almost given up on having a child when they received the awesome news that they were expecting twins. She had a difficult pregnancy and ended up on bed rest for the latter half of the pregnancy.

Prior to the pregnancy, Kat had been up for partner at her firm. As a woman in a male dominated firm, she had worked very hard to climb the ladder. She was concerned that taking so much time off would hurt her chances of making partner, but she tried her best to ignore her fears. She knew that her rest

LaToya Jenkins

was necessary for the health of the twins.

Kat rested well, and at 38 weeks she delivered two happy and healthy baby boys. She loved on them for three months at home before tearfully returning to work. She missed her babies from the moment she left them with the nanny, but she was ready to get back to work.

Just as she had feared, her shot at becoming a partner with the firm had been jeopardized by her long absence. Kat didn't give up. She knew it would take a lot of time and effort to restore her position, but she still believed it was possible. She arrived at the office early and stayed late most days. She took on a huge caseload. She attended all the social events to stay top of mind with all the partners. When she wasn't sacrificing time with her family, she was overexerting herself in trying to make up for it.

On a good night, she was getting only four hours of sleep. Her mind was foggy from processing so much information and for having to be present all the time. Kat rarely had a quiet moment to think about anything that wasn't related to a case or something one of the kids needed. She started forgetting things. First it was small things like where she put her keys or a case file. But gradually, she was so mentally drained that she began forgetting bigger and more important things.

One day after coming home from a doctor visit with the twins, Kat pulled up into the garage and shut off the car. She stepped out, closed the door, and walked into the house. She visited the restroom, sat on the couch, opened her laptop and began responding to emails. She was sitting at her laptop for nearly 15 minutes when she heard her babies' screams coming from the garage. She had forgotten them in the car!

She jumped up, ran out to the garage, grabbed them from their seats and brought them inside. Thankfully, the babies were okay. As she sat there with them in her arms, she investigated them for signs of distress. All of a sudden, tears started streaming down her face, and she knew something had

CHAPTER FOUR

to change.

When Kat first came to me, she was burned out. Her mental energy tank was nearing empty every day. She was giving out so much and not taking the time to refill. Together we devised a plan for her to take the mental breaks she needed to refuel and give her mind a chance to rest. We called them grace breaks. She started weaving several mini grace breaks into her day, during which she spent 10 minutes meditating, listening to calming music, or just removing herself from her priorities.

Weekly, she decided to spend a few hours doing relaxing activities that removed her from having to process information, like getting massages or playing golf. Eventually she let go of her fear of not making partner and dropped her caseload down to a more reasonable amount of work. Ironically, easing the demands on herself reduced her stress and made her a more likable person in the office. A few months later, she made partner.

REFILLING YOUR TANKS

Your physical, mental, and emotional energy levels should be thought of in terms of 'tanks'. We don't have an endless reservoir of energy. There are energy boosters, and there are energy drainers. What things are you doing or not doing or thinking or feeling that are draining your tanks? What things are you doing, thinking or feeling that are boosting your tanks?

Think of the moments when you feel most energized. Maybe it's when you are eating well, exercising and/or getting 7-8 hours of sleep. Maybe it's when you are engaging in social activities or investing in your personal development.

Now think of the moments when you feel most depleted. Are you harboring ill thoughts or putting bad things into your body? Are you watching or reading things that are killing your joy? You must proactively identify your energy drainers and replace them with energy boosters.

LaToya Jenkins

To successfully manage your energy, you should think in terms of daily, weekly, monthly and annual ways to boost your physical, mental and emotional energy tanks. What can you incorporate into your daily and weekly routines to boost energy? What can you proactively plan on a monthly and annual basis to reenergize yourself? Being proactive and intentional about your energy management will gain you new freedoms and peace of mind.

TIME

Some of us are married to our schedules. We draw security from our schedules. We keep multiple calendars and plan out every hour of every day, and we are completely lost if we misplace our phone or other device housing our calendars. Then there are those of us who despise schedules. We like spontaneity and the freedom to decide what to do and when to do it based on what's happening around us. We feel trapped by calendars that dictate our every move. Most of us are somewhere in between.

Whether you like schedules or not, most of us have found them necessary at one time or another. Who hasn't felt like there just wasn't enough time in the day? Who hasn't forgotten an important appointment or deadline? How often have you had to choose between doing something you loved and doing something you were obligated to do because there wasn't enough time for both? Or better yet, how often have you had to choose between doing two things that you love?

We are all given the same 24 hours each day, and we want to spend those hours living our best life. Whether you love them or loathe them, I'm here to tell you that your success in finding balance and grace in your life is largely dependent on utilizing a well-crafted, yet reasonable schedule.

When LaShawn and I first married, I was the "married to my schedules" person and he was the "despise schedules" person. Our different attitudes towards schedules weren't problematic during the first couple of years. He did what worked for him, and I did what worked for me. But as our family grew, our time started to shrink.

CHAPTER FOUR

With each new child, LaShawn and I found ourselves contending with one another for time to do what we wanted to do individually. Our second child was still a baby, and our oldest had a slew of extra-curricular activities. We were both working full-time hours at the law firm. We were sleep deprived and barely had time for one another. Work was being neglected and our kids had needs that we weren't fulfilling.

I knew that there were changes we needed to make to our schedules. As a schedule savvy person, I was excited to dig in and craft a master schedule for our family, but I knew I would have to find a way to get buy-in from my husband who was schedule resistant. There were compromises we both needed to make to benefit our family and to continue doing the things we loved and were called to do. I knew we needed a schedule that was flexible enough for my husband and secure enough for me.

After careful thought, I developed an approach to scheduling that worked for both of us. I call this approach the S.I.M.P. (Sane, Intentional, Mission-Oriented, Priorities-Based) Schedule. No matter what you've got on your plate, ensuring that your time management is sane, intentional, mission-oriented, and priorities-based will buy you freedom and peace of mind.

Sane
Make sure your schedule is reasonable and accounts for your needs and the needs of the people you are bound to. Take into consideration the way you are wired and the way your people are wired. Try to anticipate potential pressure points and look for opportunities to eliminate or minimize them in your schedule.

Intentional
I always say that if you don't have it on the calendar, don't expect it to happen. A well thought-out calendar shortens the gap between your intentions and execution. You must carve out the time to think through and capture what needs to be on your calendar. What's your plan for meals? What's your plan for self-care and family care?

LaToya Jenkins

Mission-Oriented

What is your mission? What's your purpose? What are your goals? Your calendar shouldn't be haphazard and made up of meaningless events. It should be a reflection of not only your mission, but the mission of your family. If you haven't yet developed a mission statement for your family, set aside some time to do so. Your family's mission should incorporate the strengths and callings of each family member. Your family's mission should take your entire family to the next level.

When you sit down to organize your time, you should start from your mission. Then forecast where you want to be in five years, two years, six months, next month, next week, and work your way back through the details. What you place on your calendar should propel you towards the goals of your mission.

Priorities-Based

If you love your family and value the time you spend with them, your calendar should reflect that. With five kids, it's challenging to make sure that everyone's needs are met and that everyone feels important and loved on. When we came up with a master date schedule for everyone in the family, we struck gold. Essentially, every kid goes on a parent date each month. My husband and I date one another once a week, and the two of us also take 2 days a month alone to date ourselves. We prioritize these dates on our calendar and disallow other less important things to take their place. Make a list of your priorities and order them. Does your calendar, at a glance, represent the things and the people you value? If not, you may need to re-evaluate where you are spending your time and determine which activities and/or events need to be replaced. Are you maximizing the efficiency and quality in how you're spending your time?

CHAPTER FOUR

SUPPORT

Taking the time to strengthen yourself in the areas of time management and energy management are critical to your success. But the most important key to your success is your support system. As human beings, we were not created to do life alone. We suck at it. In fact, most mammals live and thrive in communities. Take the elephant, for example. Elephants are amazingly communal. They are most certainly independent in personalities and roles. There are leaders, matriarchs, and even introverts and extroverts, but they all come together profoundly as a community. They are highly cooperative, and they work together as a team. They care for each other's offspring, defend one another and have close ties.

The greatest gift I have given myself as a wife and mother is the gift of a strong and diverse community to support me. I call this community my "elephants". If you are ambitious enough to believe you can reach the stars, you better make sure you have some elephants with you.

It wasn't until I was pregnant with my third child that I realized how great of a support system I had. I was striving and toiling to accomplish things on my own and essentially running myself ragged instead of tapping into the grace that was available to me.

I remember the moment the lightbulb switched on. I was 7 months pregnant and working from home while caring for my toddler. I was up to my eyeballs in work for the law firm – my husband's primary business – and feeling a little disenfranchised over not having enough time to work on my own business pursuits. On top of it, I was wearing myself out trying to keep up with the cooking and cleaning of our home.

Another cleaning and grocery day came around, and I spent the entire day resenting all my tasks. Against my wishes, my husband decided it was time to call the number on a housekeeping service's business card he had been saving. He must have thought it was hilarious to watch me fuss at him for providing the help I desperately needed yet refuse to seek out myself.

LaToya Jenkins

The cleaning lady arrived the following week and did an amazing job. I was so humbled that I cried. Why hadn't I thought to get help earlier? Why had I wasted so much of the time I could have been diverting to work or being with my children on tasks that weren't even important to me?

I had my priorities disorganized and I was prideful. It wasn't just the kind of pride that bound me to cleaning my own house even though it was exhausting and unenjoyable. It was the kind of pride that had me thinking I could do everything myself. I considered community a luxury and not a necessity, and I didn't need anything or anyone else to accomplish my goals. That pride was running me into the ground.

Thank God, I got the revelation that I was created as a communal being. When I did finally reach out for support, I got my joy back and was able to accomplish far more than I would have hanging out on my island.

There are three areas of support in my elephant community, and you deserve to have these as well: Delegation, synergy, and growth.

Delegation

We are only given 24 hours in each day. When you have a mountainous to-do list, those hours seem to disappear right before your eyes. It is easy to get off on an island and believe that you've got to do everything by yourself. A proverb I live by says, "A friend loves at all times, and a brother is born for adversity." You don't have to do everything yourself, and in fact, only pride would keep you in bondage with that belief. Discerning when to delegate, what to delegate and to whom to delegate to is critical in removing limits and experiencing deeper levels of grace.

Take a good look at your roles and the tasks associated with each role. What are the things that only you can do? What are the things you enjoy doing? These are the things you keep on your to-do list.

CHAPTER FOUR

With the rest of your list, identify the people in your home, place of business, or community who either have expertise or invested interest in something on your list or a desire to perform specific items on your list. These should be people who understand and can execute your vision. Some of these people you will hire. Some will volunteer their hands and others might be your children or other family members who should rightfully share in performing some of your tasks.

The key is finding and keeping people in place who are better than or as good as you are at performing the tasks. That might take some searching, inquiring or even training, but the goal is being able to hand off these tasks in confidence. Another avenue for delegating is locating apps or other non-human tools that will manage specific tasks for you.

Synergy
Synergy is realized when two or more people come together to create a greater effect than they would have separately. The people you synergize with are people who have a common goal. Your family should have common goals that compel each member to work together, to lift each other up and to propel one another forward. By cultivating an environment that values teamwork and the celebration of one another, your family will provide much needed synergy to support you as you support them. Your family should have an understanding of the vision and the culture needed to get there.

Likewise, seeking out friends and colleagues who are on a similar journey to rub elbows with is something to consider. You all can inspire each other, encourage each another and make each other better. Iron sharpens iron.

Growth
This area of support represents the next level entities in your life that are there to pull you up to your next level. I say entities because this type of support may come in

different forms. It may be a person, an organization, your faith, a training or schooling environment, coaching or even counseling. These entities challenge you to grow and keep you accountable. They provide the tools you need to visualize next steps and overcome obstacles.

CONCLUSION

When LaShawn and I were planning our wedding, we decided to send a video invitation instead of a traditional paper one. We recorded ourselves telling our dating story, and it was a really fun project. We took turns interviewing one another on camera.

When I asked LaShawn what he thought of me, I remember him saying I was his Proverbs 31 woman. In case you haven't heard of it, there is a proverb that speaks of a dynamic woman who is an excellent wife. She's trusted and adored by her husband and children. She takes care of everyone; her home is impeccable. She's prudent financially. She's wise and kind. She essentially manages to be everything - including gorgeous.

I could have been super flattered by LaShawn comparing me to this woman, but instead I was overwhelmed and intimidated by the thought that he expected me to live up to all of that. How in the world was I going to manage all of that? I couldn't stand that Proverbs 31 woman and what I perceived to be the impossible standards she was setting.

wThat was until I read deeper into her story and realized that she was a manager more than a toiler. She didn't toil to accomplish all she was doing. She delegated and leaned on support when necessary. She cared for herself and boosted her energy. She was a planner. She was a business woman and still valued her family. She was tapping into grace to put the puzzle pieces together.

Caring for a family while managing a career, business, or other pursuits is tough work. I applaud all of you women who have the courage and ambition to do both. I see your struggles, and I see your triumphs. I see you. And I am right here with you.

CHAPTER FOUR

Challenges will come. Such is life. But when they come, you've got what it takes to rise up to each challenge.

I believe that you can live a life of thriving and not just surviving. If you are looking for additional support or would like to discuss ways to implement the tools I've discussed in this chapter, please **visit my website at www.latoyajenkins.com** to schedule a free coaching consultation.

LaToya Jenkins

LEARN ABOUT
C. SHAUN OWENS

C. Shaun Owens, MS, affectionately known as "Coach O" has been a higher education administrator, coach, and leader in non-profit organizations. Currently, he is a professor with a passion for teaching and speaking on leadership development, entrepreneurship, organizational psychology and successful living.

Armed with lessons from his days as a football coach, Owens focuses on creating, building and sustaining High Performance Learning Teams (HPLTs). He distinctly focuses on HPLTs by teaching team members how to become Peak Performing Learning Individuals.

Owens is in the final stages of completing his doctoral degree (EdD) from Grand Canyon University in Organizational Leadership with a specialization in Organizational Development. In addition, he has two masters' degrees (MS) from Franklin University in Business Psychology and Communications & Marketing.

Connect with C. Shaun:
LinkedIn: C. Shaun Owens
Twitter: @TheProfessorOwens
Instagram: @TheProfessorOwens

Chapter Five

Unleash the Power of Practice

C. Shaun Owens

What will it take in order for you to live your best life?

I have asked this question of every athlete I have coached since 2012; what I refer to as the optimal question.

It began with a football player in his senior year of high school. He was a phenomenal athlete, but I noticed that he played to the level of his competition instead of the level of his talent. When he competed against someone really good, he left it all out on the field, but against an inferior opponent, he brought his game down to their level.

One day after practice I asked him, "Why are you afraid to be great?" He did not answer me immediately. As a matter of fact, he did not answer me for at least a week.

Later he responded, "What happens if I give it everything I have, and it still doesn't end up working in my favor?"

I respected his answer because I knew that it was coming from a 17-year-old kid who had hopes of playing Division I football but did not have any scholarship offers on the table at the time.

I put my hand on his shoulder and said, "No regrets. The reason you put it all on the line, scholarship or not, is so that at the end of the day, you can say you gave it everything you had. That's it."

Chapter Five

He looked at me and asked, "That's it?"

I said, "Yes. That's it. If you give it all you have and it does not go in your favor, you can walk away knowing that you gave it everything you had."

Have you ever been there? Have you ever had a goal that you're trying to reach, but rather than give it everything you have, your fear of failure caused you to hedge your bets against yourself so that you had an excuse if it didn't work out?

Quite often, our self-limiting behaviors are rooted in the fear that we aren't good enough.

Were you one of the smartest kids in your high school, but when you got to college, realized the world was full of smart people? Or perhaps you rode the wave of being one of the youngest managers in your company, but now that the years have passed, prodigy status no longer applies.

There are also plenty of folks who struggle just to perform at an acceptable level, with the thought of being considered exceptional as status reserved for "other people".

While mindset plays a major role in achievement and confidence building, nothing beats simply being good at what you do. If your abilities are a source of insecurity, let me introduce you to a powerful tool.

Practice.

Practice is important because as the old sports adage goes, you play how you practice. In life, we have similar references such as, "you reap what you sow" or "you get out of something what you put in". They all have the same contextual meaning: You can't expect what you haven't worked for.

In the sports arena, athletes practice every day to hone the skills to beat their opponents. The purpose of practice is to get better, to learn, and to question. Although practice can be boring and monotonous to athletes at times, a coach sees practice as the art form of perfecting skills. If you want to live a life of optimal impact, then practice must be your best friend.

Now let's break down the concept of beneficial practice into several components.

PERFECT PRACTICE

A perfect practice is not easy to accomplish, but it can be done with the right focus going into the practice session. Every perfect practice needs a few things to get the practice on target: Outcomes, everyday drills/disciplines (EDDs) and coaches.

Practice outcomes are found in a team or tribe's practice plan and practice goals. The practice plan is used to assess and account for time; whereas, the practice goals are used to measure success or failure. Practice goals - like life goals - should H.A.R.D* not S.M.A.R.T. The goals that you set for your practice should be:

Heartfelt: We feel an emotional attachment to a goal; it scratches an existential itch.
Animated: Our goal is so vividly described and presented that to not reah it leaves us wanting.
Required: A goal needs to feel as critical to our continued existence as air and water.
Difficult: A goal needs to push us outside our comfort zones and to test our limits.

Practice EDDs are used to ensure that the basic fundamentals are never lost. These everyday drills/disciplines MUST be done in order to ensure that you never forget how to do your job - no matter how talented you are.

Finally, a perfect practice needs coaches. Every great team has coaches to assist along the way. The coaches are there to provide a roadmap, feedback, and relationship. If you can find a coach or coaches to assist in those critical areas, living with

*Murphy, M. (2014). Hundred Percenters: Challenge your employees to give it their all and they'll give you even more. New York, NY: McGraw Hill Education

optimal impact will become exceptionally easy to start and maintain.

PRACTICE MAKES PERMANENT

The one thing that people must know about practice is that the time you spend practicing - whether you do it right or wrong - will become muscle memory. When fatigue sets in, you will rely

> *"Practice does not make perfect. Perfect practice makes perfect."*
> *- Vince Lombardi*

on that muscle memory. Be sure you practice in a manner that develops the skills you want to display.

Any amount of time you devote to practicing should also be done with passion and effort. When you practice with passion and effort you'll tap into the same level of performance when your next opportunity presents itself.

PRACTICE WITH PURPOSE

The reason most people get tired of practicing is because they lose focus of their objective, which could be anything from scoring a touchdown to closing a multi-million-dollar deal. Once you know the objective, set goals and milestones along the way so that you will know if you are on track.

Getting better is a gradual, chartable and measurable outcome where the desire is to get at least one step closer each day to a realized goal. Some days you may advance two or three steps, but when you skip practice, you are wasting a day that you cannot get back.

PRACTICE WITH PEOPLE

The people you choose to practice with will be instrumental in how well or ill-prepared you will be when your opportunity comes along. I had a wrestling coach who used to always say

CHAPTER FIVE

to us, "You are only as good as your wrestling partner. If your wrestling partner is good, you will be good. If your wrestling partner is bad, you will be bad."

BUILD YOUR SQUAD

Just the same, you want to surround yourself with people who will elevate your skillset. If you don't have people you can connect with in your current professional circles, mastermind groups and even meetups can be a great place to build authentic relationships.

SELECT YOUR COACHES

I talked about coaches earlier, but their ability to provide feedback to accelerate your advancement and hold you accountable to your plans can't be overstated. If you have more than one skill that you want to develop, you may want to have more than one coach who can help guide you towards each goal. However, if you have more than one coach, I think it is critical to know which coach's voice is most important. On every athletic team, there are multiple assistant coaches, but everyone knows who the head coach is. Make sure your coaches know who the "head coach" is.

FIND YOUR CHEERING SECTION

Everyone needs a support system who roots for you, but all voices are not created equally. Fans are people who genuinely care for you and will always be there with you. Cheerleaders root you on because when you win, they win. Groupies on the other hand can make your feel good, but they always have their hands out looking for something. The danger in surrounding yourself with groupies and not fans is that one day you will look around and they won't be there. You must also beware of hellraisers. They may appear to be cheering for you, but it may simply be a distraction to get you to lose.

When times get challenging, the cheers of your fans may be exactly what you need to motivate you to keep pressing toward your goal.

C. Shaun Owens

CALL TO EXECUTION

Create your own daily practice plan using the following practice plan outline for several weeks. Monitor how many days were winning days and how many days were losing days. If you use this small sample set for several weeks, you can then assess if keeping that same pattern will lead to reaching your objectives.

Remember, you are always practicing until you get an opportunity, and once the opportunity presents itself, how you practiced will show up and hopefully pay off.

PRACTICE PLAN OUTLINE

Write down your One Word: Choose and write down a personal word that is your annual focal point. This should be a GOD word not a good word. This word will not change for 52 weeks so choose this word wisely (*Suggested reading: One Word That Will Change Your Life by Jon Gordon, Dan Britton & Jimmy Page*).

Write Your Overarching Goals: List no more than 3 H.A.R.D. (Heartfelt, Animated, Required, Difficult) goals. Goals are long-term constructs and take time to acquire and accomplish. An analogy I like to use borrowed from Sean Covey is, "landing the plane". If you are a pilot your goal is simple, land the plane safely.

Write Your Supporting Daily Objectives: Write down aligning actions to be taken - no more than 2-3 things you MUST do each day. I refer to the objectives as "the critical and mandatory things that need to be done to land the plane". Objectives are short-term actions that are required in order to achieve your overarching goal. If objectives are not accomplished, you will not win the day.

Write the Best Tactics: These are designed and specific actions that you have to complete in order for the Supporting Daily Objectives to be reached. Tactics are the things you do daily. They are often referred to as habits or rituals. If tactics are not

CHAPTER FIVE

done constantly and consistently, daily objectives become very hard to complete.

Write and Say Positive Affirmations: List 3-5 positive affirmations on an index card that will help you focus and motivate you to complete your practice plan. Say them 3-5 times a time a day as well as anytime you feel fear, anxiety or confusion creeping into your mind.

Write Down Your Lessons Learned: At the end of the day, list 3-5 things you learned as a result of trying to accomplish your daily practice plan.

Calculate Your Scoreboard Outcome: Tally your Daily Objective and Tactics. If you completed them all, you win. If not, you lose. If you win enough days, you will win the week. If you win enough weeks, you will win the month. If you win enough months, you will win the year. If you win enough years, you will win the decade. If you win enough decades, you will win in life.

The ultimate goal to win in life and it starts by making a goal and a checklist to ensure you win more than you lose (or learn for those who endorse positive psychology).

In conclusion, I want to reiterate the importance of investing in your practice time wisely because practice in and of itself does not produce the best of anything, only perfect practice does that. Not everyone will commit to optimal impact living because it does require lots of dedicated practice and a big investment of time.

And remember, don't simply practice; practice perfect, practice with purpose, and practice with good people, because in the end what you practice is what becomes permanent.

C. Shaun Owens

LEARN ABOUT
ERICKA YOUNG

Since founding Tailor-Made Budgets in 2005, Ericka Young has served hundreds of happy clients, helping them pay off more than $2.5M in debt.

Ericka is the author of *Naked and Unashamed: 10 Money Conversations Every Couple Must Have*. She teaches her message of debt freedom through her e-newsletter, personal coaching, workshops and speaking engagements.

After college, Ericka took an expected path in her degreed field of engineering. During this time, Ericka and her husband Chris carried loads of debt that included student loans, car payments, and a mortgage. They were doing the things that all young couples do, but along with that came added stress.

It was during this time that The Youngs discovered Dave Ramsey's program. Within five years, Ericka and Chris dug their way out of nearly $100,000 in debt and Ericka realized that her true passion was not in engineering, but helping others gain control over their money through financial coaching.

Her love for numbers and data crunching translated easily into analyzing financial information. She became a certified financial coach by Dave Ramsey's Lampo Group and is now a recognized expert in financial coaching.

Ericka is a frequent media contributor for TV, newspaper and

Chapter Six

online publications. Learn how she can help you get your financial house in order and subscribe to her free weekly financial tips at TailorMadeBudgets.com

Connect with Ericka Young:
Website: TailorMadeBudgets.com
Facebook: @TailorMadeBudgets
LinkedIn: Ericka Young
Twitter: @BudgetsByEricka

Four Keys to Making Your Money Behave

Ericka Young

Money is said to be the number one cause of the stress that Americans face. By simply reading this chapter you are taking control of your life in such a way that not only will it help you reduce debt, but it will also leave you with more money at the end of the month. Gaining control over your money will allow you to get better sleep, and yes, it will even allow you have more fun.

My husband Chris and I paid off over $90,000 worth of debt, which led me to start my own consulting business where I can help people just like you get rid of their debt, organize their finances, and live a truly financially free life.

While coaching more than 300 families, I've created a formula that is easy to start and makes personal finance bearable for those who dread the thought of facing it.

There are four keys to the process:

- Set realistic goals.
- Have a financial reality check.
- Create a balanced budget.
- Find your debt-free date.

Over the next few pages we will dive into each of these concepts individually so you can finally have a road map to freedom.

Chapter Six

KEY #1: SET REALISTIC GOALS

While the world's most successful people know that setting goals and writing them down is a key to success, frequently quoted studies estimate that only 3 out of every 100 adults write down their goals. In fact, only 14% of people even have a goal in mind!

In chapter 3, Shawnté Jones laid out a master plan for goal setting, so you can't say you don't know how to do it. If you plan on creating a healthy financial life, you must set goals for yourself on a regular basis.

What is a goal?

There is a difference between a dream and a goal. Dictionary.com defines a dream as "a cherished hope, ambition, or aspiration." A goal is "the result or achievement toward which effort is directed."

It is time to turn your dream into a goal. No more wishing and hoping. Let's put some effort towards those most important desires in our lives.

All goals need to have 5 components. The must be specific, measurable, attainable, relevant and time-bound; in other words, they must be SMART.

When it comes to your finances, here are six steps to setting and more importantly, achieving your goals.

1. Identify your goals and get in agreement about those goals with anyone in your life that they will affect.
2. Prioritize your goals by importance.
3. Determine the dates for completion/achievement.
4. Estimate the cost for achievement by doing some research.
5. Decide how much money you currently have available to spend on each goal, if applicable.

CHAPTER SIX

6. Determine how your goal will be achieved. Will you work overtime? Will you get a second job? Will you cut expenses in certain areas? How much will be saved towards the goal in the monthly budget?

Start with identifying no more than 2 or 3 financial goals. Make sure they are SMART goals, and work through the six steps for each goal. This will put you on the road to success!

KEY #2: HAVE A FINANCIAL REALITY CHECK

There is nothing scarier than looking in the mirror in the morning after a really bad night! But if we don't, we won't see the unruly hair, food remnants in our teeth or stains on our clothing. Once you've set goals, it is time to face the facts about where you are currently. In order to clean up a mess, you must first be able to see it.

One of the most common issues leading to financial problems is not knowing exactly what's going on with your money. Many people have no idea what the exact balance is in their bank account, let alone other accounts in their name. They aren't sure exactly how much they owe, either.

In fact, while borrowers typically know their balance on debt like mortgage or car loans, according to NerdWallet's 2015 American Household Credit Card Debt Survey, actual lender-reported credit card debt was 155% greater than borrower-reported balances.

Some reasons for the discrepancy could be that consumers don't report balances they intend to pay off or they haven't checked their balance in a while. They may also be embarrassed by the actual amounts they owe. Even with a discrepancy that large, it's reasonable to see that most people just don't know what they owe at all. It is time to figure out exactly what you owe and know your balances.

To do this, pull out all of your bank and lender statements. And I do mean ALL of them, including:

- Latest checking and savings statement
- Credit card statements
- Mortgage statement
- Retirement accounts (401k, 503b, IRAs, other stock investments)
- Other loan statements (including student loans, car loans, etc.)

Review them all to know what you have and what you owe. Write all of this information down to keep it organized for future reference.

It can be difficult to look at these numbers, but know that this first step is the most important in making positive changes. Do not pass any judgment on yourself. This exercise is not to make you feel guilty or bad about the decisions you have made. It's simply the first step in taking control and facing your reality.

KEY #3: CREATE A BALANCED BUDGET

I said it – the dreaded b-word! According to The Millionaire Next Door written by Thomas Stanley and William Danko, more than half of all first-generation millionaires follow a budget. So if you want to know the path to wealth, start by following their lead.

Having a budget is a scary thing for a lot of people, but it doesn't have to be. In fact, budgeting can be fun. After all, what's more fun than starting to see that you have the money to take care of everything you need and perhaps even have some left over?

Creating a budget can be intimidating, but let's get started with a few simple steps:

1. **Develop a budget mindset.** Think about why you haven't had a budget so far. Acknowledging why you haven't had one is the first step to making one. Think about that and then decide that you are going to move past the issue to create a budget. Taking action can

CHAPTER SIX

break the cycle.

2. **Understand the common budget mistakes.** These include the following:
    - Not working or using it every month.
    - Having an incomplete budget.
    - Not getting every family member involved.
    - Not creating a zero-based budget.
    - Leaving out the fun.
    - Not creating a spending plan.
3. **Make commitments.**
    - Use cash so you don't overspend.
    - Stop using credit cards so you can get out of debt.
    - Find ways to save money so your budget stays on target.

Creating a budget that works for YOU is one of the most important tasks in accomplishing your financial goals.

Now let's get down to business.

Remember when I talked about how writing down our goals gives us a better chance of achieving them? Well next we are going to write a budget so you have a better chance of sticking to it.

There are many budgeting tools available. You can use an app, download a spreadsheet, create your own, or stick to pencil and paper. Whatever you choose, make sure it is written and visible.

Here's how to get started:

- Tally your total net monthly income (income minus taxes), and take into account all sources of income such as paychecks, child support, alimony, pension, social security, etc.
- Determine ALL of your expense categories and include your due date and financial obligation for each

category. You should have your previous months' bank statements on hand plus current month's bills and any notices of obligations that apply for this month to complete this step.
- Total your monthly expenses and then subtract your total monthly income. The goal is to have a balance of $0.

If you have a positive balance (money left over) then dedicate excess to paying off debt or savings.

If you have a negative balance (not enough money), reevaluate how and where you are spending your money.

You might need to eliminate some non-essentials to balance your monthly budget.

See how simple that is?

It may sound like a lot, but you will feel better instantly when you create a detailed and balanced budget and start seeing the wins from working it. I promise!

Give yourself a few months to get the hang of it. Inevitably, you will forget a bill. You may overspend on clothing. You will even get tired of trying. However, if you are consistent, you will learn how to make the budget a healthy part of your financial life.

KEY #4: FIND YOUR DEBT-FREE DATE!
One of the biggest traps we can put ourselves in is to only make the minimum payments on our debt. We believe that one day we'll magically have more money, and then we can pay more. It seems like a great way to stretch the budget, but the reality is that it only makes the problem worse.

If you only make the minimum payments, interest will continue to add up, and this will make your debt liability much greater. You'll be digging a deeper hole. This results in you staying in debt much longer than necessary.

CHAPTER SIX

The best and more effective way to get rid of debt is to create a debt snowball. Dave Ramsey first coined this method, and finally other financial gurus adopted it as well. The Debt Snowball will help you organize your current debt from the smallest to largest balance, and it helps you pay them off in an efficient manner. When used correctly, the Debt Snowball helps you facilitate how and when your creditors will be paid in full.

Here's how to do it:

1. First, you want to list all of your debts, including the total balance and minimum monthly payments.
2. Find the one with the lowest total payoff amount and determine a proposed new monthly payment based on your budget.
3. Next, calculate what the payoff date will be if you continue to pay that amount.
4. Once you've paid it off, it's time to move that "extra money" (both the money you were paying on the one you paid off and the extra you shifted) to the next lowest debt amount.

You'll continue to do this until all of your debts are paid off. Going this route will result in less interest and less time in debt, and ultimately, you'll experience freedom!

I suggest you take this exercise a step further and calculate the date you will be free of all your debt. Add up the number of months to pay off each debt, and then determine when that will happen in real time. This is your debt-free date.

Sticking to a plan to get out of the debt is probably the most challenging step of all. This is because it typically takes the most determination and stamina, but it is the most rewarding step of all. Just think about all of the things you can do, places you can go, and lives you can impact if you don't have debt dragging you down.

Now go get free!

Ericka Young

LEARN ABOUT
ELAINE
CAULEY

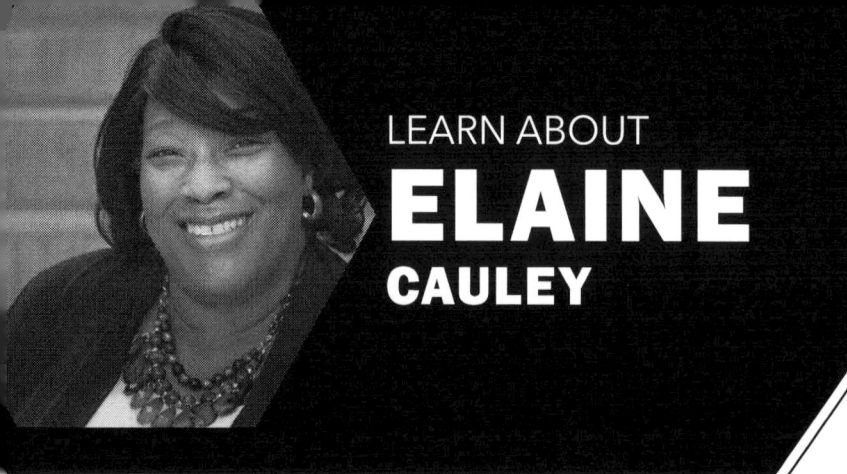

Elaine Cauley has a passion to serve people dealing with grief. She's spent more than 30 years helping people work through the pain of losing a loved one and now she's helping them think ahead by equipping them with the tools to create a legacy plan.

Through her books, workshops and consulting, Elaine helps people overcome the fear, overwhelm and procrastination of making their final arrangements. She wants us to recognize that much like births and weddings, death is a part of life that we should plan for. Elaine works with individuals and families to get everyone on the same page to prevent the drama that tears families apart.

Elaine is the author of "My Will Be Done! Preserving Your Legacy" and the companion workbook, along with the personal memoir, "Birds Really Can Fly". Elaine teaches workshops across the country for churches, community groups and funeral homes and provides resources to those who frequently encounter grieving families.

A Chicago native, Elaine retired from the United States Postal Service after 28 years with 18 years in management. She proudly wears the titles of mother, grandmother, great-grandmother, sister, friend and volunteer.

Chapter Seven

Connect with Elaine Cauley:
Website: ElaineCauley.com
Facebook: Elaine Cauley - Author

Preserving Your Legacy: More than Money and Memories

Elaine Cauley

What's going to happen when you're gone?

That's a question most people don't want to think about, let alone discuss. It's as if planning for your death somehow hastens it. Maybe you tell yourself, "I'll be dead anyway, so it doesn't matter what my family chooses to do." Although that may sound like a reasonable approach, it doesn't account for the stress we pass along to our loved ones.

I remember sitting on a bench comforting a woman who had just lost her father. On top of the grief, she had to deal with a family feud over his final arrangements. I felt helpless as I tried to console her.

Watching people host car washes and sell chicken dinners to pay for a funeral breaks my heart. Life insurance or putting money away for your final arrangements may seem like an expense you can do without if money is tight. But take a moment to think about the burden you will leave your family. Is that the last memory they will have of you when they reflect on your life's journey?

When you're gone, your loved ones should have the time and space they need to deal with the loss without the extra pain of trying to figure out what you would want them to do, dealing with disputes or acting as referees between feuding family members. Love your family enough to make the decisions for

Chapter Seven

them so all they have to do is deal with the grief.

Over my lifetime, I've found myself drawn to helping people who are grieving. I began seeking out more and more information to help them not only deal with their emotions, but to address other concerns they were facing. Many of those concerns involved working through final arrangements and distributing the possessions of their loved one because the deceased didn't clearly make their wishes known. I have found in most cases that it wasn't that the person didn't want to be better prepared for their transition; they simply didn't know where to start.

After volunteering for many years, I formalized my efforts by creating books, workshops and other resources to help people think about and plan for the legacy they want to leave when they're gone. In my book, My Will Be Done! Preserving Your Legacy, I walk people through scenarios and give them practical steps to get their affairs in order. If you haven't left your loved ones a clear plan to follow, pay close attention to this chapter.

WHAT'S YOUR LEGACY?

Your legacy is more than a price tag. Your legacy brings laughter to the faces of others, joy to their hearts, memories to their spirits and reflections to pass on to future generations. A financial crisis or personal disaster can wipe out your home, car and bank account in the blink of an eye, but a true legacy endures.

Cambridge Dictionary provides multiple definitions for legacy, including the following:

- Anything handed down from the past, as from an ancestor or predecessor
- A situation that has developed as a result of past actions and decisions, and
- Something that is a part of your history or that remains from an earlier time.

CHAPTER SEVEN

When we look at our legacy through the eyes of others, they can include things like:

- Photographs
- Family recipes
- Jewelry passed down from previous generations
- Clothing or other items that hold sentimental value like your wedding dress, cap and gown or class ring
- Your Bible

You notice that I didn't mention bank, real estate or cars. Legacy or wealth is not always established in the form of money. Even if you don't own any of the things typically classified as "valuables" you still need to make plans.

THOUGHTS FOR ENTREPRENEURS

You've invested years of hard work into building and growing your business. What will happen to all you've created when you transition from this life? There are considerations like developing an exit strategy for your business not just for your death, but even if you become incapacitated. What will happen to your book royalties, copyrights, patents and other revenue-generating assets?

If you are the sole business owner, it's critical to designate someone to act on your behalf. You don't want to be incapacitated with no one to handle the day-to-day needs of your company, like paying the bills and making payroll. Have you considered who will be able to manage your website, social media accounts and banking?

There is so much we take for granted because we are doing it capably today, but being prepared can eliminate a lot of undue stress and protect your assets. If you already have an exit strategy, does it cover incapacitation and death? Don't give your business to the government or let it go bankrupt from legal fees and disputes.

LEGACY THROUGH CHARITABLE GIVING

Are you connected to a cause that you want to continue supporting after you're gone? There are so many one-time or long-term gifts that you can donate instead of letting your family battle with the courts. Here are a few ideas of how some people have chosen to support non-profit organizations after their transition.

- If you are an artist, you can leave your unsold paintings.
- If you are a songwriter or singer, you may want to leave your unpublished songs.
- If you love animals, you could leave money to help provide food for an animal shelter.
- If you are a writer, you may want to leave your copyrights to set up a library.

> ***Love your family enough to make the decisions for them so all they have to do is deal with the grief.***

CONNECTING YOUR LEGACY AND PURPOSE

It's easy to get so caught up in the activity of day-to-day life that we forget about the purpose of it all. Purpose is a word that is often used lightly, but it has the capacity to make a huge difference in the lives of those that you leave your legacy to.

By thinking ahead about the legacy you want to leave, you have the ability to live beyond your life on earth. When you live beyond yourself, you live with intention, and you're not leaving key decisions for others to make after you're gone. You realize the choices you make today can affect future generations – for better or worse.

Here are some action points to help you begin your journey of creating a legacy plan. Keep in mind that I'm not an attorney, and these suggestions are totally based on my personal experience in helping families and having communication with attorneys.

CHAPTER SEVEN

As you complete these items, I want you to keep in mind that you are creating an atmosphere that will allow those loved ones to focus only on healing after your passing. Love them enough to do this for them!

1. Identify an accountability partner who will ensure that you complete the steps of the process. This may be your spouse if you are married. You can get a lot more accomplished when you have someone that is supportive and on the same page as you.

2. Take time to list all your assets and designate each to someone. Remember that the price tag isn't the determining factor. Consider all items - great and small - like pictures, journals, books, jewelry, wedding dresses, and of course, your house, car, business and financial assets, if applicable. Don't be afraid to ask your loved ones if there are certain items they would like to have. What they value may surprise you.

3. Put your wishes for your final arrangements in writing. Do you want to be buried or cremated? Do you want to prepay or establish an account to pay? Who do you want to speak at your service? Do you have a color you'd like to be buried in, or that you'd like your family to wear? Are there certain songs or scriptures you want included?

4. If you're married, sit down with your spouse, and share transition wishes with each other. This should not take the place of putting it in writing.

5. Make sure you put all your important papers in a secure location, including an electronic application like Google Drive or on a USB Drive.

I want to make it easier for you to create your legacy plan with a free resource to help you get organized. Visit **www.ElaineCauley.com/download** to receive your free copy.

Elaine Cauley

LEARN ABOUT
YUBEKA
RIDDICK

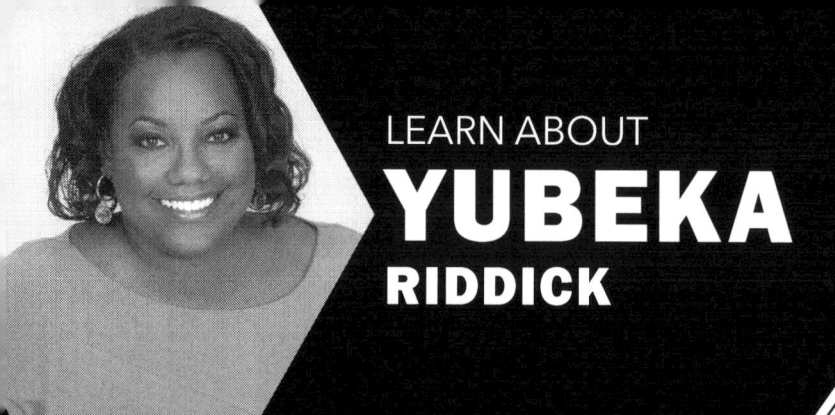

Yubeka Riddick is a personal identity expert and founder and CEO of BNOTCONFORMED, an organization that is missioned to help adult and teen women develop and discover their God-given identity. Her varied background as well as her personal struggle of seeing herself the way God sees her provides the perfect foundation as she equips others to avoid an identity crisis.

Yubeka is the author of Authentically You: Unveiling Your True Identity as a tool to help individuals unlock their identity by taking them on a journey of personal experience, scripture, and wisdom. Authentically You is being used in book clubs and small groups across the country.

A licensed and ordained minister, Yubeka is also a graduate of Syracuse University. She is a native of Brooklyn, New York, lover of shoes, and currently resides in Jacksonville, FL with her husband Lawrence and their daughter, Cherith.

Connect with Yubeka Riddick:
Website: bnotconformed.com
Facebook: @identitycrisisaverted

Chapter Eight

Putting an End to People Pleasing

Yubeka Riddick

Once upon a time there was a little girl who had so much to say. Sadly, she felt like people didn't listen to her. When she expressed thoughts contrary to popular opinion, it made the people around her very uncomfortable. So, the little girl learned to be quiet.

As she grew up, it became the norm for her to keep her opinions, thoughts, and ideas to herself. She wanted to be known as the girl who was outgoing, smart, and kind, but more importantly, she wanted to be someone who got along with people.

To the detriment of her own health, she avoided saying "no" out of fear of hurting other people's feelings. If it needed to be done, she was on it. All. The. Time. "Yes" was her default response even if she had other things to do; she would make it work because the need for approval outweighed the need to say "no".

Does this person sound familiar? Do you recognize her deep down on the inside of you?

I was this little girl. Even as I became a grown woman, saying "yes" became so easy – even when it wasn't. I had this need to be loved, valued and validated by others, and in my mind, the easiest way to get all of those things was by becoming all things to all people. I wanted to make everyone happy because

Chapter Eight

their approval made me feel good about myself. I could go home and say, "Hey, Mr. or Mrs. So-and-So likes me. I did a great job...go me!"

In reality, I was still looking for value, love and acceptance from other people instead of the one person who could give it to me unconditionally. I was stuck in a prison of my own making; performing just so I could be recognized. All the while, I didn't know I was empty on the inside. There was a hole on the inside of me, and I kept thinking that all of these other people would fill it and keep it filled. But it didn't work out that way.

What happens when the kudos go away? What happens when the opportunities to showcase your skillset disappears? Who is it that looks back at you in the mirror when it's just you and silence? Who are you without resounding cheers or words of validation? Who are you when you are left alone with your thoughts?

In those moments, we are forced to come face to face with ourselves. And to be honest, sometimes that's more than we want to deal with. We run from ourselves by hanging out with friends, binging on television and even getting involved in relationships that don't serve us well. This is all because we don't want to look in the mirror and deal with our issues. My motto was, "Let's avoid this at all possible costs." It's uncomfortable. It hurts. I don't want to deal with me.

CONSEQUENCES OF PEOPLE PLEASING

How many times have you decided not to pursue an opportunity, make a major move or decision because you weren't sure if your family or friends would support or cheer for you? I know I'm not the only person who had second thoughts about moving outside of my comfort zone because I was afraid of what other people would think.

Another consequence of people pleasing is shrinking who you are so that others can feel better about themselves. At no time did Jesus stop being God in order to make the masses feel better about themselves. God doesn't stop being God

CHAPTER EIGHT

because people don't believe in Him. He continues to be who He is in spite of how people feel about Him. Whether they believe that He exists or doesn't, that He is all powerful or not, or if He has control or doesn't, He is still God.

Have you lost your voice? You know that you should speak up, but you don't because you're afraid that people will disapprove or not validate your opinion?

People pleasing can also lead to being taken advantage of by others because you don't want to hurt their feelings or say "no". Please understand that I am in no way saying go around and hurt people purposely. But there are others who will take advantage of you always saying "yes", even if it means you don't agree or may not want to do what is being asked.

HOW DO YOU MOVE BEYOND PEOPLE PLEASING?

It took me moving across the country alone twice in order for me to finally realize that I was a people pleaser. Through the assistance of sound biblical counseling and self reflection, I got free. The first thing I had to do was learn how to say "no". In Bible school, one of my instructors said something that resonated with me so deeply that I share it with people I work with all of the time. The instructor said, "No is a complete sentence."

There is no need for a qualifier or an explanation because no is a complete sentence. Once I grabbed a hold of this concept, I was on my way to freedom. I was free to give that little girl back her voice and to let her know that her opinion matters.

Learning how to say "no" is one of the most important steps you can take. I remember the first time I told my extended family "no". You would have thought I grew two heads and cursed them out! They had not seen the "new" me, and the expectation was that I would go along and not speak up like I had been doing all of my life. Well, let me tell you, when you get a taste of what it's like to not have to fit into other people's expectations of you and when it's not an expectation you have of yourself, you become bold enough to not be moved by their response. Needless to say, I stood firm with my family that day and every time since then. Whether they like me or not, they respect that I will no longer go along to get along.

The second thing that helped me gain freedom from people pleasing was to overcome the need to perform to gain approval. What would happen if you only performed for an audience of one - your Heavenly Father? My heart belongs to Him, and He is the One that I have to please. Once I realized who I was in Him through Christ, the desire for approval, acceptance, value and validation shifted from people (who were bound to let me down) to Him, the one who would always be there for me. I seriously became a "Daddy's Girl". My value was now affirmed by my Father, who loves me with an everlasting love.

Being a people pleaser places you last on your own list. I was always available at the expense of my time, finances, and even my mental and physical health. I know I can't afford to go to this particular event because I have only enough gas to get me through the week until payday, but so-and-so asked me to help out and I already said "yes". I know I should really take this Saturday to rest, but they need volunteers at church for this event, and I should be there. This is people pleasing. It's knowing that you should say "no", but instead you say "yes" to the detriment of yourself so that other people can make you feel better.

But you have to get out of people pleasing and do what's right for yourself. You have to have that freedom and that new confidence. It's knowing that if I decide not to attend the event, my Heavenly Father still loves me. It's being aware that I don't have to prove my worth to others by my service. Performing for an audience of one means that I can go to bed at night with ease knowing that I said "yes" to all of the things God has asked even if it meant that I said "no" to what others asked of me. Realizing who I was in Christ led to a shift in the desire for approval, acceptance, value and validation from others to finding those things in Christ. This shift was healthy, forgiving, and true.

CHAPTER EIGHT

In those silent times of looking at myself in the mirror, I would ask God, "Do you see me? Do you value me? Do you accept me?"

And His response was, "Of course. I created you. You are loved, and you are mine". I was filled with such amazement and joy in knowing that I am seen, valued, and affirmed by God Himself. Acceptance from the people around us can be highly subjective and ever-changing. I no longer had to seek approval from others because I had been approved by God.

Now, when opportunities present themselves, I don't stop and think about what my family or friends will think. Recently, an opportunity to enter full-time ministry was presented to me. First, I had to ask myself if this was an opportunity from God. Then, I had to discuss it with my husband because it would affect my family. We had a 3- month-old at the time, and the opportunity would mean moving across the country and uprooting our lives within a few months.

Now, had I still been a people pleaser, I would have talked to a slew of people to ask their opinion. I would have thought about the effects of us moving on everyone else without focusing on what not moving would have meant. If the people that I loved and trusted would have said "no", I would have seriously considered staying in Phoenix. It would have been to the detriment of my mental, spiritual, physical and emotional health. I would have placed the weight of others above what I knew in my heart God wanted for us as a family.

5 STEPS TOWARDS FREEDOM

Now you may be saying, "That sounds good, but I'm not there yet. I'm still dealing with being a people pleaser." Let me give you some concrete steps to take towards finding freedom.

Step One: Practice saying the word "no". Yes, I'm serious. Every day for a week, when someone asks you to do something and you know you cannot do it, tell them "no". If an opportunity doesn't arise in seven days, continue to say "no" until you have done it seven times.

Step Two: Write on a sticky note, *"No is a complete sentence."* It doesn't require an explanation. Post it throughout your home, and make it your screen saver or locked screen on your phone, computer, tablet, etc. You need to see this phrase everywhere you look for at least two weeks.

Step Three: Ask God to show you who you are by praying and reading the Word of God. But don't ask Him about the "you" that you think you should be to make everyone happy. Ask Him to show you the unique individual that He created. Ask Him to show you YOU.

Step Four: Find one scripture in the Bible that affirms your identity in Christ and memorize it. For example, you can look at Colossians 2:7 which is about you being complete in Christ.

Step Five: Seek professional counseling if dealing with trauma or emotional wounds that feels like it is too much to overcome on your own.

I would love to hear from you as you begin taking steps to becoming free from people pleasing. Let me know how the journey is going by emailing me at **info@bnotconformed.com**. You are not alone, and I look forward to hearing about your progress.

LEARN ABOUT
KELLI CENTER

Kelli Center is a Licensed Professional Counselor and the owner of Centered Living Counseling & Coaching Services, LLC.

Kelli is passionate about helping individuals to become mentally and spiritually whole so they can be free to live their best life. She feels especially called to bridge the gap between the spiritual and mental health communities, dispelling misconceptions that keep people of faith from receiving the support necessary to meet their mental and emotional needs.

With more than 15 years of experience, Kelli works with individuals, couples and families from all socio-economic and cultural backgrounds. She has experience in addressing an array of needs, including depression, anxiety, relationship communication and trauma.

Kelli also provides Christian counseling, as well as supervision and training for other counselors seeking independent licensure.

Connect with Kelli Center:
Website: CenteredLivingCounseling.com
Facebook: facebook.com/kcenterLPC
Instagram: @kellicenter_lpc

Chapter Nine

Living Your Best Life is an Inside Job

Kelli Center

We live in a social media saturated world where people post the best representations of themselves for others to see. "Living my best life" is a common phrase, usually accompanied by pictures of people working out, eating a healthy meal or spending the day at the beach. Yet, we also live in a dichotomous time where mental illness – including depression and anxiety – seem to be at the forefront of many conversations. Suicidal incidents make a regular appearance on daily news shows and blogs, and they involve everyone from celebrities to elementary school students.

As a counselor, I'm often tasked with helping people find their balance, live an authentic life, face problems as they arise and reach a place of contentment. To start, we must redefine what it means to "live your best life." I believe that living your best life includes being mentally, emotionally and spiritually whole.

MENTAL WHOLENESS

Everyday, people find themselves facing obstacles that they are unsure of how to navigate. This leads to feeling overwhelmed, which is often categorized as Anxiety or Depression in the clinical setting. When you spend too much time focusing on the future or looking forward, you can experience symptoms of Anxiety. Conversely, when you spend too much time thinking about the past or looking backwards, you can experience symptoms of Depression. Common thought patterns for

Chapter Nine

the anxious mind might include "what if" phrases, whereas depressed thinking patterns may include "should have, could have, would have" statements.

It is estimated that people spend an alarming 90% or more of their time in one of these thinking spaces, either in the past with regret or in the future with uncertainty and fear. The problem with these thinking patterns is that they both lie in a space of time that is not in our control. Chances are, there is nothing that you can do to change events or circumstances that took place in the past nor are you likely to be certain about the circumstances in the future. The only space of time that we are able to control is the present.

Therefore, the best way to combat anxious and depressed thinking patterns is to focus on the present moment. Although I realize that this concept is easier said than done, the first step is to recognize that these negative and unhealthy thought patterns exist. The next step is to take action.

In order to combat anxious thinking, you can do the following:

1. **Stay in the Present Moment** - Don't allow yourself to play out the "what if" or "should have, could have, would have" narrative.

2. **Focus on What's in Your Control to Change** - After you identify what's in your control, create a task list to begin to accomplish your goals. How do you eat an elephant? One bite at a time! Make your goals small and attainable so you don't become overwhelmed.

3. **Fight Fear with Fact** - Anxiety is fear based. When we focus on things in the future that are not in our control, we become anxious. I always suggest that the best way to fight fear is with fact. Identify what the truth of the situation is and focus on that.

   For example, someone may say, "I'm afraid that I won't have my direct deposit in time, and I will get evicted because I can't pay my rent by the deadline."

CHAPTER NINE

The anxious person might become fearful and start to play out scenarios where he is homeless and living on the street. This can be fought by identifying the facts. He can call the landlord, explain the situation and intentions to pay, and find out how long the grace period is before a late fee is charged or eviction proceedings begin. Then, whenever those thoughts try to re-enter his mind about being homeless because he couldn't pay rent on time, he has the facts to focus on. He can focus on the fact that he has a 5-day grace period and that his landlord is aware that he will be late this month.

Sometimes our brains need to hear us speak that truth. You may need to open your mouth to combat the negative thoughts. You could say, "It's ok. I have until the 5th and even after that point my landlord knows I will be paying rent. I will not end up homeless." Remember, combat anxiety-producing fear with fact.

4. **Don't Isolate Yourself** - The depressed mind will encourage you to be alone. This only gives those negative and depressed thoughts room to grow. At its worst, this may even lead to thoughts of suicide or feeling like things would be better if you weren't here. This is a commonly reported thought amongst those who have battled Depression. Know that this is the mark of an unhealthy mind. If you experience these thoughts, reach out for help immediately! Contact a friend or family member who you feel safe sharing your feelings with.

5. **Seek Professional Help** - If you are experiencing symptoms of Anxiety or Depression, I recommend that you follow-up with a healthcare professional to be evaluated for counseling and other treatment options. I understand that sometimes people are hesitant to seek medical and professional help for mental health concerns. You may feel "weak" for seeking help or afraid of what others may think about you. However, this isn't something to white knuckle your way through.

Kelli Center

Get the help you need. This doesn't mean that you are crazy and it doesn't mean you will be receiving this help indefinitely. If you had a physical pain that wouldn't go away, you would seek medical attention. Mental and emotional pain shouldn't be any different.

EMOTIONAL WHOLENESS

Emotion is defined as, "a natural instinctive state of mind deriving from one's circumstances, mood or relationship with others." It's important to amplify that our emotional stability is connected to our interactions with other people. Even though emotional wholeness encompasses so much more, I want to focus on this element within relationships. These tips are primarily focused on married couples, but you'll find that most are applicable to any close relationship that has the potential to experience conflict.

Over the years, I have counseled many couples and if I could sum up their problems into one primary concern, it would be poor communication. It is the root cause of many disagreements that lead to conflict and even divorce. Everyone wants to be heard and we all want our feelings validated. In an effort to do so, we end up talking over each other and as the saying goes, "when our mouths are open, our ears are closed."

Sometimes relationships look a lot like an old western quick draw shootout. Each person turns their back on the other, walks 20 paces and turns, aiming to be the first to fire a shot. Before you know it, both people have their defensive walls up that they use as a barricade to shield themselves as the shots are being exchanged. Your home becomes a battlefield with insults as the heavy artillery. Loneliness and neglect become the wounds and all involved are hurting. It becomes increasingly difficult to maintain the facade of a happy home. It's draining. You feel unheard, unloved and defeated. It is at this juncture that many consider divorce.

An estimated 40% of all first marriages and 60% of second marriages end in divorce. People often think that if they get a new partner, things will be different. Initially, they may

CHAPTER NINE

be different; but as time goes on and the newness of the relationship wears off, you may feel like you're trapped in a scene from the 1993 movie, Groundhog Day, reliving the same arguments you had in your previous relationships.

Rather than exiting the marriage or relationship, try to repair it by increasing positive communication and having healthy interactions. No relationship or person is perfect, and they all require effort.

The following tips and tools can increase positive interaction and communication in your marriage and other relationships:

1. Use an I-Message
As I mentioned earlier, everyone wants to be heard and have their feelings validated, but our intended message often gets lost in the mess of our emotions. We may yell, cry or go off on tangents unrelated to the issue at hand. This confuses the listener and in turn they'll likely begin to defend themselves against claims, which causes you to continue to feel unheard. Don't succumb to the pressure to pull out your hair and scream; instead, try using an I-message as a means of directly communicating your feelings.

I-messages generally contain the following four elements:

 a. How I feel about the behavior and its effects.
 b. A description of the behavior – what actually happened.
 c. The actual concrete and tangible effects of that behavior on you.
 d. The behavior you would like or prefer.

Another way you can express an I-message is as follows:

 a. I feel *(identify and state your feelings, label the emotion)*
 b. when you *(describe the action that affects you or relates to the feeling)*

c. because *(explain how the action affects you or relates to the feeling)*
   d. and I would like it if you *(explain your suggestion on how the behavior can change)*.

Example:
   a. I feel frustrated *(how you feel)*
   b. whenever you are late picking me up *(description of offending behavior)*
   c. because it causes me to be late for my job *(concrete effect on you)*
   d. and I would like it if you were more punctual *(the behavior you would prefer)*.

2. Put a 3x Focus on Yourself

Here's an exercise to try with your partner: As you're sitting down and directly facing each other, both of you take your hand and point your index finger at the other person. While doing so, look down at your own hand. You should notice that although your index finger is pointed in your partner's direction, your pinky, ring and middle fingers are pointed towards yourself. This is a friendly reminder that we should examine our own actions three times as much as we examine someone else's actions. A notable Bible passage says to remove the plank out of your own eye before pointing out the speck in your brother's eye (Matthew 7:5).

It's always easier to identify what someone else did wrong and what behavior they need to change, but it's more beneficial to identify what you did wrong or could have done differently. Although it may be more challenging, doing so will be more rewarding.

Next time you have a disagreement with your partner, I challenge you to identify at least three things you could have done differently in the preceding events without focusing on their actions or using the word "but". This will immediately lower the other person's defenses, and it will cause them to reflect on their actions. They will likely return the sentiment, pointing out what they could have done differently as well. In the end, each person leaves the encounter feeling heard and validated.

3. Focus on Forgiveness

When you have a disagreement or argument, don't wait for the other person to apologize first. Be quick to forgive. Holding on to offense, holding grudges and being angry is unhealthy. I've heard unforgiveness described as eating a poisonous apple and expecting the other person to die. Not only does it feed discord in your relationships, it also releases toxins into your body by putting you into fight or flight mode for extended periods of time. Unforgiveness not only creates emotional discomfort, it can also have a negative impact on your physical health.

4. Seek Couples Counseling

It may be initially uncomfortable to talk to someone else about your problems, but most couples I've worked with report feeling a sense of relief once they engage in a counseling relationship. It can be very helpful to have an unbiased person listening to both you and your partner. Both of you will feel like you have a voice, while learning skills to increase positive communication at home. The result? Decreased emotional distress and increased satisfaction in the relationship.

SPIRITUAL WHOLENESS

Spiritual wholeness encompasses more than one's ascribed faith or belief system. It includes the overall balance you have in life. When you are spiritually out of balance, it undoubtedly affects every other area of your life.

We live in a fast-paced world where we work long hours and get minimal sleep so that we can have the greatest output of our time and energy, generally with the hopes of having financial gain or obtaining a desired goal. It's about doing more with less, particularly in the United States.

This busy, fast-paced life often causes us to neglect ourselves and our spiritual needs. We wake up consumed with problems and the cares of the world, and we crash at night going over our to-do list for the next day. When we are not spiritually in tune and connected, we may find ourselves running on empty; depleted of all energy with nothing left to give to others or ourselves. Spiritual wholeness is about pouring back into yourself, refueling, centering yourself and finding inner peace.

THE TALE OF TWO ME'S

I remember having a vision years ago of me making my way through a tall grass field to the pearly gate in heaven. My dress had rips and tears in it and my hair was a mess. There was dirt on my clothes, face and hair. My exposed legs, face and arms had streams of blood from the scratches I endured while trudging through the field. I was tired and out of breath from the journey.

As I stood before the gate, panting with my head down, I mumbled, "I'm here Lord. I'm here." As I glanced over to my left, I saw another woman also standing before the gate. This woman was clean and well put-together like she had a fresh shower. Her hair was combed. She was smiling from ear to ear, twirling her dress, and dancing with excitement. I suddenly felt bewildered as I compared my appearance to the other woman. I asked the Lord why we were so different, and He replied, "You never learned to rest in Me." As I looked closer, much to my amazement, I realized that the other woman was me as well!

My takeaway from this vision was that we have a choice in how we live this life. We can live a peaceful life, or we can live a rough, unsettling life full of anxiety, where we work by the sweat of our brow. It's not just about getting the job done or reaching a goal, it's about how you get the job done and how you reach the goal. I believe the better way is to live a life like the woman to my left; the "me" that learned to rest.

Neglecting our spiritual rest can also lead to sickness and

CHAPTER NINE

disease. Many years after that vision, I was in my early 30's, a single mother working full time, starting my own business and serving in leadership positions in two Christian organizations. I thought I was doing good work, even though I was stretched beyond my capacity. I often functioned off of little-to-no sleep and soon found myself at the doctor's office where I was diagnosed with Shingles. I was told that although the Shingles virus lives in anyone who has had Chicken Pox, it generally lies dormant, plaguing senior citizens as their immune system weakens. For someone my age, Shingles is very rare and is generally triggered by stress.

There are many ways to refuel in your pursuit of spiritual wholeness, including:

- Spending time in prayer or meditation
- Quiet reflection
- Journaling
- Hiking
- Exercise or Yoga

Regardless of how you decide to refuel, the most important thing is that you do.

As you can see, living our best life is more than taking a few pictures at the perfect angle for social media. It requires intentionality. It takes some work, but the work is worth the reward.

Don't expect yourself to navigate every challenge alone. Utilize the support of a counselor, therapist or other mental health services to help you through the process.

Kelli Center

LEARN ABOUT
La'Vista
JONES

La'Vista Jones, CLBC helps business owners bring order to the chaos of life and business. She believes the price of success doesn't have to include burnout and broken promises to yourself. By discovering a better way to run your business, you can get back to making yourself and what you love a priority.

As an author, speaker and community builder, La'Vista is leading a movement of business owners who want more from life than frazzled days and sleepless nights. Her unique magic is adding time back to your day by streamlining processes, identifying operational gaps and outsourcing. Her creative approach to business analysis and implementation saves her clients valuable time that they can then spend on their own self-care routines.

An Ohio native, La'Vista currently resides in Arizona with her husband, their son, 'The Cub' and fur baby, Bull Dozer.

Connect with La'Vista Jones:
Website: LaVistaJones.com
Facebook: facebook.com/lavistajones
Instagram: @lavistajones

Chapter Ten

The Cost of Chaos: What Are You Willing to Pay?

La'Vista Jones

We've all heard it - that catchy cliché when we've worked ourselves past the edge of exhaustion, overloaded our production capacity, set the bar too high and fallen victim to the comparison trap once again.

You've got to pay the cost to be the boss.

But what exactly is the cost? Blatantly ignoring our physical needs because we're too prideful to take a break? Being perceived as on-edge because we're operating from an emotional space that is out of balance? Experiencing professional sabotage because our personal capacity is stretched beyond a sustainable pace? Those are pretty high stakes, but what if there was a better way?

There is a way to accomplish your ambitious vision, grow your business and live your best life, and it starts by taking care of your greatest asset – You.

A LOOK IN THE MIRROR

Self-care is not a new phenomenon and neither are the effects of ignoring it. However, entrepreneurs are greatly impacted by a lack of self-care and so are their businesses. Burnout has become so common that it was recently classified as an occupational phenomenon by the World Health Organization, and far too many of us have paid its hefty price.

Chapter Ten

One of my favorite self-care scripture references is Mark 12:31 which says, "Love your neighbor as yourself" (NIV). At its surface, it instructs us to love our neighbors. However, I believe that it also teaches the importance of loving ourselves first. Once we set the foundation to treat ourselves with care, love and respect, it will become second nature to extend the same graces to others.

Here's a self-care lesson I had to learn the hard way:

The pending birth of my son caused me to face a lot of uncertainties. How well would I adjust to motherhood? Would my inexperience with children affect me bonding with my baby boy? Would I ever get my cute pre-pregnancy nose back? But one thing I felt confident about was my ability to continue to rock out in business and serve my clients just as I had pre-baby – even if that meant even earlier mornings, more frequent late nights and grinding harder than ever to get everything done. I was literally working on client deliverables at 3:00 a.m. on the morning my son was born (Disclaimer: I no longer support #TeamNoSleep)! I was convinced that since my solopreneur grind hadn't really been affected during my pregnancy, it wouldn't be affected once I came home with my little miracle, either.

I've never been more wrong in my life.

As a business owner that has a solid understanding of personal capacity, I had a sub-contractor on deck to fill in for me. She had been debriefed on all my client deliverables so she could step in whenever I needed her support. The major flaw in that plan is that I never actually intended to need her. My real plan was to show everyone just how much of a boss I really was, perfectly balancing everything all on my own.

I soon found out that motherhood is just as tiring as it is rewarding, especially in those first few months of around the clock feedings, unregulated sleep schedules and important bonding time. The new demands that came with my new role

CHAPTER TEN

as a mommy coupled with maintaining my marriage and my home while trying to grow my business left very little time for anything else. In fact, there were days I couldn't figure out the last time I had even showered. But still, I kept telling myself that I could handle it all on my own. This was me paying the cost to be the boss.

As a result, I was exhausted. I wasn't sleeping. I was missing deadlines. I was canceling business-related calls that I hadn't had time to prepare for. I was neglecting critical tasks that I just couldn't fit in. I wasn't enjoying precious moments with my son because I was so stressed out about everything that was piling up on my to-do list. I wasn't eating well. I was battling against post-partum depression. I wasn't exercising. I was beating myself up each time I walked past the bonfire-sized pile of laundry and other household chores that were left undone. I'd broken the promise to my husband to prioritize our quality time together. I wasn't attending church. I wasn't even praying.

I was barely existing, and I was completely overwhelmed. I was merely running off of adrenaline rushes from each urgent situation that required my immediate attention. My quality of life sucked to put it mildly, and I wasn't prioritizing my own care.

And then it happened. I got an email that I knew was coming:

Hi, La'Vista. As much as it pains me to do so, I need to terminate our contract.

As I read on, all I could do was cry. Every single word in my ex-client's email reflected just how out of control, unstructured and chaotic my life was. My conscious decision to handle everything on my own was adversely impacting me physically, emotionally and mentally. It also had a detrimental ripple effect to those connected to me, and it was even hurting the marketplace itself. In that moment, I finally realized I was experiencing burnout, and I knew that I desperately needed things to change.

The beauty of chaos is when it forces you to reorder your

priorities. And that shift in my priorities had to start with my self-care routines.

THE COST

I define burnout as what happens when we spend too long trying to avoid being human and ignoring our own needs.

Looking back, there were clear signs that had burnout written all over them. While the list below is not exhaustive, it does highlight some key warning signs that I noticed in hindsight. If I would've paid attention to those signs as they were happening, perhaps things wouldn't have gotten so bad. Maybe I would still be working with that client I lost.

- **Running on empty** – simply having nothing else to give. The truth of the matter is that in that season of burnout, even if I wanted to do more for myself, my family or my clients, I couldn't. My physical and mental resources were depleted; I was tapped out. This happened primarily because I didn't prioritize my own self-care.

    Many entrepreneurs postpone self-care because they are stuck in hustle mode in their business. This is counterproductive because you can't make money if you're knocked out of the game by burnout because taking care of yourself didn't seem like a priority.

    I started my rebound by identifying and implementing some simple, but key routines for myself. I started getting up in the morning and going for walks around my neighborhood. I started taking the time to paint my nails again. I insisted that daily showers were a non-negotiable (ask any new mama...this was a game changer). Most importantly, I started taking off my super-mommy cape and asking for help when I needed it.

- **Loss of enjoyment** – the inability to enjoy activities or moments that you would normally find exciting. I knew that I was dealing with a serious problem when I found

CHAPTER TEN

myself sitting on the couch as I held my newborn, looking down at him with no feelings of joy.

This was the little boy I'd spent years praying for. So when the joy left and the happy emotions seemed to suddenly dry up, I knew that was a major red flag. I also lost enjoyment in my work. At that time, none of the normal tasks or projects that I normally loved working on elicited any type of emotional response from me. And the relational care for my clients suffered as well to say the least.

Focusing on self-care helped turn things around for me, and eventually I started feeling like myself again. I started to fully enjoy my new normal of juggling my responsibilities as a wife, boss and mother.

- **Trouble focusing** – being easily distracted and overlooking details. With the operational oversight that my company handles for many other business owners, having trouble focusing yielded a lot of damage control that needed to be done. My lack of focus actually increased the amount of work I needed to do. I had problems prioritizing deliverables and executing much of anything.

I paid a high price for the chaos that I let creep into my life. I became stuck, and my family and business suffered.

WHERE ARE YOU ON THE BURNOUT SCALE?

Do you see yourself in any parts of my story? Are you feverishly grinding out the vision at the sake of the visionary?

My company, *31 Marketplace* was established in 2005 because I saw a lot of business owners living in chaos and burning themselves out trying to live out their big vision all alone. They were without a structured plan, and they were neglecting their essential needs like rest and personal connection.

Determined to keep people from walking a mile in my burnout

La'Vista Jones

shoes, I now take a more holistic approach to business sustainability, from focusing on establishing operational strategy to reinforcing consistent and purposeful self-care routines for the business owner.

I believe that the greatest impact in the marketplace is made by fulfilling the vision as well as taking care of the visionary.

Take this short assessment to gauge how close you may or may not be to entrepreneurial burnout.

On a scale from 1-5, rate the below statements (1 - being 'seldom true' and 5 - being 'mostly true').

___ I feel drained of physical or emotional energy.
___ I think negatively about my business.
___ I am harder on people than they deserve.
___ I am easily irritated by small problems within my business.
___ I feel unappreciated by my clients.
___ I feel that I have no one to talk to about business.
___ I feel that I am achieving less than I should.
___ I feel under an unpleasant level of pressure to succeed.
___ I feel that I am not getting what I want out of my business.
___ I feel that I am in the wrong business.
___ I am frustrated with many aspects of my business.
___ I feel that gaps in my business impact my ability to do a good job.
___ I feel that there is more work to do than I have the capacity to complete.
___ I don't have time to do many of the things required to run a quality business.
___ I find that I do not have time to plan things out as much as I would like to.

_____ TOTAL

CHAPTER TEN

Assessment Key
15-22: No sign of burnout
23-38: Little sign of burnout
39-53: At risk of burnout
54-68: At severe risk of burnout
69-75: At very severe risk of burnout

If you're greatly experiencing any of the above statements, it is time to step back, take a deep breath and take action towards living a better life.

A MINDSET SHIFT ABOUT SELF-CARE

Even after reading my story and seeing the cost that I had to pay, you may still have some limiting thoughts when it comes to your own self-care and I want to address those.

Self-Care is selfish. Yup – and it should be. But it's time to once and for all let go of the guilt associated with using your time and resources to take care of yourself. Think of all the roles you play in a day. If you're anything like me, you're a son or daughter, a sibling, a significant other, a parent, a business owner and then some. If you're running on empty because you haven't taken the necessary time to recharge and pour into yourself, eventually you'll have nothing left to give to those you care about.

But let's be clear, your self-care is not about being able to take care of others; it's a critically fundamental way to take care for yourself simply because you're you!

I think it's safe to say that we've all heard the catchy phrase, 'in case of an emergency, secure your own oxygen mask before assisting others.' Well, getting selfish about your self-care is about putting on your own oxygen mask, simply because you need to breathe. Period.

Self-care is too expensive. If you're a business owner, you can't make money if you're sick or dealing with burnout. Taking yourself out of the game because you've neglected your physical needs is a cost that is too expensive to pay. Self-care

La'Vista Jones

doesn't require a weekly pampering session at a 5-star resort, but it does require consistent and purposeful actions to care for yourself – a lot of which you can do at no cost.

Self-care takes too much time. I love this quote by Jack Kornfield. "If your compassion does not include yourself, it is incomplete." Start where you are. Set and maintain realistic expectations about your time. Even if you can only budget 20 minutes a day on self-care, extend grace to yourself to enjoy and make the most of the time that you have.

Right now, you might be thinking to yourself that you don't even know what to do for self-care. If so, let me introduce you to a simple process that you can start implementing today.

THE S.P.A. METHOD

The S.P.A. Method helps you infuse self-care into your day. Ideally this process takes an hour to complete, but that hour can be broken down into 20-minute segments and enjoyed throughout the entire day. Let's walk through it step by step.

S - Do something SMART

During this 20-minute segment, focus on your mind. Do something that expresses your creativity or stimulates your intellect.

- Watch a TED Talk
- Solve a crossword puzzle
- Read a book
- Paint something
- Research/ learn a new skill

P - Do something PHYSICAL

Focus on your body during this 20-minute segment. Do something that challenges or supports a physical need.

- Walk to your neighborhood park
- Practice yoga
- Take a nap
- Try a healthy smoothie recipe
- Play with your pet

CHAPTER TEN

A - Do something AFFIRMING
Take 20 minutes to focus on your spirit. Do something that encourages you.

- Buy or make a bouquet of flowers
- Meditate and pray
- Create an affirmation for yourself
- Write yourself a love note
- Chat or schedule a date with a friend

NOW WHAT?

Okay, so you've got a game plan for your self-care, but that doesn't do anything about the reality of the chaos going on within your business. The presence of chaos and the feeling of being overwhelmed means that you need more structure.

A lot of the conversations I have with new clients are initiated because they have the desire to hire an assistant. They feel that hiring someone in a support role will help resolve the chaos they are experiencing in the day-to-day operations of running their businesses. While I'm a supporter of getting the right help for your business, I've found that hiring an assistant isn't necessarily the best next step in bringing order to that overwhelming chaos that is familiar to so many. In my experience, I've found that the idea of a new hire can sometimes be replaced by fully utilizing a tool instead, which is usually much easier on your monthly budget.

Think about it: If you hired an assistant today, would you even know what you'd want them to do? And beyond the tasks you'd want to delegate to them, do you already have documented processes in place that outline the expectations and preferences you'd want them to deliver on?

As I said earlier in this chapter, I believe the first step in accomplishing your ambitious vision and growing your business while living your best life is through consistent self-care. The next step is building a solid operational foundation for your business, with self-care routines infused throughout.

La'Vista Jones

If you scored high on the burnout assessment, I'm pretty confident that you're feeling overwhelmed in your business on a daily basis as well. I want to help you close the gap between the vision you have for your business and the actual execution of that vision. I want to help you turn all the noise going on in your head into a structured, realistic plan that you and your current or future team can follow.

It's time to create solutions to overcome the obstacles that currently have you stuck. Let's walk through the S.M.A.R.T.E.R.™ framework I created and use with clients to strategize beyond those obstacles. Here's a brief summary of that framework.

S - Seek Help
A big part of seeking help is getting clear about the obstacle or problem you want to address. You may even need help figuring out what that obstacle may be. If there are multiple items you need to focus on, prioritize them and start gaining traction- tackling one thing at a time. Remember to give yourself permission to accept the right help when it's offered and get comfortable being transparent enough to ask for help when you need it.

In business, this may look like hiring a coach like myself to help you navigate your journey or joining a mastermind group.

M - Map It Out
Create a strategy or life plan. This is where you identify the steps needed to get from where you are now to where you want to be. I suggest starting with the big picture, then move on to adding in the details. Remember, a solid strategy has measurable milestones and realistic time frames to hold yourself accountable to.

A key to successfully implementing a plan is writing it out. There is just something magical that happens when you put pen to paper.

CHAPTER TEN

A - Be Accountable
Accountability shouldn't be likened to a four-letter word. Instead, accountability should be embraced because it ensures that you get to do your most meaningful and important work in the marketplace. Also, being accountable to another person or group helps you establish boundaries with your time and energy while getting to see yourself make traction towards your vision. Be mindful to celebrate your victories during this phase to build your momentum to keep going!

I have a business bestie that I meet with every other week, and she definitely helps to hold my feet to the fire. She is tough on me when she needs to be, but she celebrates my victories like they are her own.

R - Utilize Resources
Take inventory of your resources - the tools, trainings, organizations and people around you. Then be mindful of the best way to utilize (not use up) those resources to work towards your goals.

For sustainable growth, business owners should consistently cultivate and utilize the resources around them through the spirit of collaboration, not consumption.

T - Build Trust equity
This might be Ene of the harder steps because it often involves relying on others to do things for you. Trust equity with others is built over time, but its foundation is established by being a person and business partner of integrity that other people know they can trust.

E - Evaluate Your Life Harmony
Take time to do periodic pulse checks of your life to identify any areas that may need a bit more attention than others; then make the necessary adjustments. Also, be sure to extend grace to yourself. The goal is progress, not perfection.

R - Establish Routines
If you don't already know them, identify and get familiar with

La'Vista Jones

your core love languages. Based on your core love languages, begin to implement self-care routines that fluently speak your most dominant languages. These routines need to become non-negotiables in your life, and that takes consistent, purposeful practice.

The S.M.A.R.T.E.R.™ framework is a fluid and repeatable process to help you develop and implement the solutions you need for the life and business that you want.

It's easy for overwhelm and chaos to take over when you're trying to run a successful business and live a fulfilling life. But who wants to live with overwhelm and pay the cost for chaos?

I work with solopreneurs that desire putting an end to the overwhelm and chaos while infusing self-care into their life and business. If that's you, I invite you to download your copy of **SELF-ish: A #RescueRitual Guide to Prioritize YOU in Your Business** today. It's a free guide to help rescue yourself from overwhelm by implementing structure and reclaiming your time so you can prioritize yourself in your business at the top of your to-do list. Visit ***www.LaVistaJones.com*** to download your free copy today.

LEARN ABOUT
Dr. Will
MORELAND

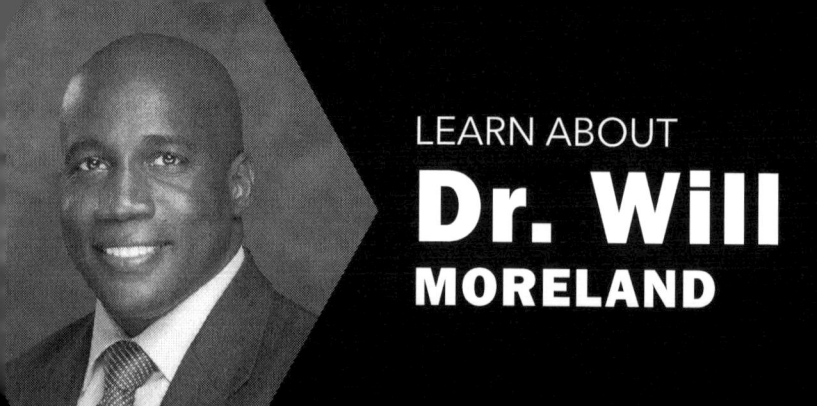

Dr. Will is on a mission to impact, inspire and influence society in a meaningful way.

Raised in one of the roughest cities in America, Dr. Will's upbringing in Compton, California included gangs, drugs, murder and an incarcerated father. Throw in low self-esteem and a speech impediment, and you have the beginning of Dr. Will's journey.

After many tough years in California, Dr. Will made the choice to join the Army. It was in the military where he began to transform his life. Committing himself to personal development and education, he earned his doctorate degree at 27. After completing his service with an Honorable Discharge, he realized he was passionate about helping others discover the power of leadership and personal development that reshaped his destiny, and he launched his own company.

For the past 15 years, Dr. Will has traveled to over 40 different countries to train leaders and organizations, written 50 books and received multiple awards for his work in mentoring, business and professional speaking.

He has been married to his beautiful wife Dr. Kristie for 20 years, and they have two wonderful children - Karah and Champ. The Morelands have called Arizona home since 2010.

Chapter Eleven

Connect with Dr. Will Moreland:
Website: DrWillSpeaks.com
Facebook: @drwillspeaks
Instagram: @drwillspeaks
LinkedIn: Dr. Will Moreland

How Losing Myself Helped Me Find Myself

Dr. Will Moreland

For as long as I can remember, I just wanted better. A better quality of life. Better clothes. Better shoes. A better financial situation. Just better everything.

Growing up in Compton was interesting. To the outside world it was a horrible place, but to me it was home. It was where Grandma was waiting for me when I would come home from Caldwell Elementary with my big sister and cousin. It was the place where we would have Christmas dinner. It was the place I would learn many life lessons. The house was filled with people and filled with love.

The only thing that was missing was an abundance of financial resources. It seemed like we always had just enough. Just enough food. Just enough gas. Just enough money to pay the bills with nothing left over. Just enough!

This made me focus on money. At the time, I thought money was my biggest problem. Strangely enough, I don't remember my family ever talking about the lack of money; I just knew we didn't have it. When picture time came around at school, I can remember asking my mom if I would be taking school pictures. She would never say yes or no, but on the morning of picture day, she would hand me a twenty-dollar bill to get Package A, the smallest package. Package A consisted of one 8 x 10 photo, two 5 x 7's and eight wallet-sized photos. Just enough. It's funny what you remember from childhood, isn't it? Picture day

Chapter Eleven

is one of those memories I will never forget because I always wanted Package D - the big package. Now that I think about it, Package A was a good choice because I would not want too many of those pictures from back then floating around.

As I look back on those early days, I realize I missed out on a lot of great lessons. One of the major lessons I missed out on was learning more about what a phenomenal woman my grandmother was. My grandmother died when I was 12, and although I have some great memories, I missed the true essence of who she was. Now that I am older, I realize just how special she was.

I didn't understand how dynamic it was for a single black woman to own her own house, as a child. This was in the late 70's and the Housing Rights Act in America had just passed in 1968. And on top of that, this was the second house Grandma had purchased in California. I would love to go back and have some conversations with her and to peek into her mind. One of my biggest regrets in life was not having more meaningful conversations with her.

So why am I rambling on about the lack of money growing up, picture day and my Grandma? I'm glad you asked, because it's what most of us do in life. We focus on, pursue and worry about things that really don't matter in life, and then we miss out on the most important things in life.

Mark Twain said, "The two most important days in your life are the day you were born and the day you find out why." Many of us attribute our birth to our parents' relationship, whatever that may have been. But few people find out why they are walking the planet, why they wake up each morning or why they have been given the breath of life each day.

THE ENCOUNTER

For me, this journey started some years ago, but I remember it like it was yesterday. I woke up like any other day and started my morning routine. I went to the bathroom to wash my face and brush my teeth. As I looked in the mirror, something was

CHAPTER ELEVEN

different. I recognized the face, but I didn't know the person. I mean I looked the same, but I felt lost. As I looked in the mirror, I saw my face covered with labels.

I saw all the labels I had been called my entire life: Son, brother, friend, husband, father, mentor, athlete, soldier, gangbanger, drug dealer, pastor, veteran, black man. There were so many labels that it was like someone stamped my entire face. I was in my early 30's at the time and I was fairly successful by most people's account. But I didn't know who I was.

For the last 30 years or so, I just went along to get along. Many times, I was doing certain things because that's what the people in my life expected me to do. I was a young black male being raised in Compton. They told me that I was supposed to be a gangbanger, so I became a gangbanger. I went to church. They told me I was supposed to be a preacher, so I became a preacher. I could run fast. They told me I was supposed to be an athlete, so I became an athlete.

Up to that point, you could call me the great chameleon. What you couldn't call me was fulfilled. I didn't have a horrible life; I actually enjoyed what I was doing and carved out a pretty good life doing it. I had a great family, the big house and the fancy cars. I went on the best vacations and the whole nine yards. Most people would have traded their life for mine in a heartbeat.

One of the hardest things is to be successful at something that doesn't fulfill you. It's easy to just settle in and build a life around whatever seems to be working. Then one day we look up and we are too fearful to disrupt the life we have built - even though we are unfulfilled.

As I looked in the mirror that day, I knew something had to change. I had to change. It was the scariest time of my life because I knew my change meant change for a whole lot of other people. Most importantly, it would mean change for my family.

Over the next several months, I struggled with taking the first

Dr. Will Moreland

step toward the change I knew I needed. For the most part, I was afraid because I didn't know exactly what the change was or what it would look like. Was it not working as much? Was it changing what I did? Was it moving? I had no clue. I just knew I needed to find out who I was. Why was I here on earth?

THE CHOICE

I decided to go on what I now call a "Clarity Journey." I can tell you, this is what saved my life. This is what has bought me the joy I experience every day. This is the key to living your best life. Right before I began my "Clarity Journey", I came across this poem that became my daily motivation and inspiration. It's a simple poem, but very dynamic. The poem was written by an Italian poet by the name of Guillaume Apollinaire. It simply says…

> "Come to the edge," he said.
> "We can't; we are afraid," they responded.
> "Come to the edge," he said.
> "We can't; we will fall," they responded.
> "Come to the edge," he said.
> And so they came.
> And he pushed them.
> And they flew."

This poem resonated with me so much. I was afraid. I did think I would fall, but at the same time, I knew I would never forgive myself if I didn't at least try. I didn't want to live or die with regrets. I decided I was going to discover who I really was.

Up to this point, I didn't know if I really liked chicken or if I only liked it because that's what Grandma cooked every Sunday after church. I didn't know if I liked rap music or if I only liked it because I grew up in Compton with Ice Cube and Dr. Dre. I didn't know if I liked skiing or not because I was told black people don't ski. I needed to find out who I was, and I was determined to find my mission.

It finally came down to me having to make a huge decision. At this time, I had lived in Germany for the past 15 years. I loved

CHAPTER ELEVEN

living in Germany and thought I would be there at least another 15 years or so. But this "Clarity Journey" I was ready to embark upon meant it was time to leave Germany and move back to the United States. Other than a few pit short pit stops when I was in the Army, I hadn't lived anywhere except California and Germany.

Once I spoke with my wife, we settled on moving to Arizona to start this new journey. Mind you, we had never lived there, and we didn't have any connections. I was simply motivated by my desire to find out who I was and why I was created, and Arizona felt like a good place to start.

After moving to Arizona, I challenged myself to try new things. I wanted to travel with purpose. Normally, I would only think business when I traveled and would never take in the sights of any new city I visited. I would tell myself that I was on a mission and that I had no time for all that.

But now that I was on my "Clarity Journey", I was going to give myself the opportunity to explore and experience the world around me. For the next 18 months, I tried it all. I visited different places, ate different foods and opened my mind to seeing what this world really had to offer. I also asked myself the tough questions.

The three main questions I asked myself while I was on my "Clarity Journey" were:

1. What do I want to do the rest of my life professionally?
2. Who do I want to do it with? What clients would I work with?
3. If I went back to doing what I was doing before, would I be happy?

These three questions became my anchors at the time. What I knew about life then and even more today is that tomorrow isn't promised to us. From the time we are born to the time we die, we have a limited amount of time. When you look on a tomb stone, you will see two dates – the day a person was

Dr. Will Moreland

born and the day a person dies. Separating those two dates is a dash (-) and your life is that dash. What are you going to do between those two numbers?

We live in an amazing world, but very few get to experience even a fraction of it because they have chosen to settle in life. They have chosen to exist instead of live. I wanted to live.

During my "Clarity Journey", I went snow skiing, jet skiing, camping, horseback riding and I even attended a few NASCAR races. I ate escargot, alligator and I did the unthinkable and tried brussels sprouts!

What I began to realize more and more on this journey is that I was living the opinions and experiences of other people with no actual investigation of my own. This is true for most of us. Think for a moment. Your home city and state were chosen by your parents. Your initial belief system was shaped by your parents. The subjects we learned in school were determined by someone else.

If you are like me, what you are passionate about or have a desire to do wasn't even taught in school. I didn't know I could travel the world and impact lives. There was no school course called "Impact Lives 101". There was no degree offered called Bachelors of Transformation. I had to choose from what was offered to me, but I had to discover what I was born to do.

During my time of discovery, I kept reflecting on those same three questions.

1. What do I want to do the rest of my life professionally?
2. Who do I want to do it with? What clients would I work with?
3. If I went back to doing what I was doing before, would I be happy?

I did some deep soul searching. After all, I didn't want to waste the small amount of time I had left on this planet. Even at life's

CHAPTER ELEVEN

longest span, it's still just a blink.

After I got a good sample size of new experiences and did some more reflective work, I had an idea of how I wanted to live out the rest of my life. I knew what I wanted to do. I knew the kind of people I wanted to do it with. I had found the space where I would be most happy. It was clear that for the rest of my life I wanted to IMPACT * INSPIRE * INFLUENCE * society in a positive way and help others find true fulfillment in life. Several years after my initial "Clarity Journey", a few things have evolved. I have a deeper understanding of my purpose and mission. And I suspect this will happen for you as well. You will find ways to go deeper in the work and legacy you desire to leave.

THE RESULT

I now travel the world teaching a concept I call "Living from Your C.O.R.E." This acronym has helped shape my life and has challenged thousands of others to find their C.O.R.E by going on their own personal "Clarity Journey". These four letters stand for:

- Clarity
- Opportunities
- Relationships
- Experiences

If you are going to live your best life, first you must become clear on who you are and what you like to do. What makes you come alive? What puts the biggest smile on your face? What fulfills you? What gives you a sense of meaning in life?

I truly believe we are all put here on this earth for a reason, and it is our duty to find out why. Once you find out why, then sell out to that reason. This doesn't mean you need to become Oprah Winfrey or Martin Luther King Jr. You just need to brighten the corner of the world you were assigned to.

When you are clear on your purpose in life, whether that is helping stray dogs find homes or building the next space ship to explore other planets, you will then want to find the right opportunities that will allow you to do what you love.

Let me interject this bit of wisdom: You may discover that what you are passionate about doesn't pay much. I am often asked about this when I share my concept of "Living from your C.O.R.E." My suggestion is to lean on the education you have received or a skill you have to finance your quality of life, and on the weekends and with your available time, do the things you are passionate about.

As an example, you might be educated in the area of accounting, but you are passionate about working with the youth. Allow accounting to finance your life, and look for opportunities in your community to work with youth.

Next, you want to discover who you want to enjoy life with. This involves your personal and professional relationships. Relationships play a huge part in how you enjoy life. The people we choose to involve ourselves with can create either heaven or hell on earth. This is true for both types of relationships.

When you think about it, the best and worst times of your life most likely involved people. Your greatest joys probably involved people. Many people live miserable lives because of the people they choose to surround themselves with.

During my "Clarity Journey", I did an inventory of the relationships I had involved myself in. This process allowed me to fortify some existing relationships and walk away from others that were not healthy for me. People play an important part in our lives. Make sure you have the right ones in your life.

Lastly, you have to think about how you want to experience life. We are currently living in the best time ever known to mankind. What we are capable of and able to do is just amazing to me. I can have lunch in Phoenix and dinner in New York all in the same day. I can talk to anyone in the world with the small device I carry in my hand each day. I have been blessed

CHAPTER ELEVEN

to travel to over 40 countries and 30 states. This is not an opportunity I take for granted. Merely 50 years earlier here in the United States, I would not be able to travel as freely as I do today.

Just like any other country, America is not perfect. However, I choose to focus on what is possible and challenge what needs to be challenged in an appropriate manner. If you are reading this book, I would dare to believe that you have many opportunities that you are just not taking advantage of. No one can convince me that we do not live in a wonderful time and a wonderful place called Planet Earth. I challenge you to explore more of this amazing world. Get out more. Do more. Experience more!

As I travel now, my desire and mission is to challenge individuals to "Live from their C.O.R.E." Growing up, I realized I missed out on some great opportunities, like getting to know my Grandma Polly better. I'm determined not to make that mistake again. I'm determined not to lose who I am. I never want to look in the mirror again and not know who I am looking at. Going on my "Clarity Journey" and discovering my C.O.R.E. has been the key to living my best life.

I hope that you will venture out on your own "Clarity Journey" and find your C.O.R.E.!

Dr. Will Moreland

LEARN ABOUT
LAURIE
BATTAGLIA

Thought leader, writer, speaker, and transformer of people, cultures and workplaces, Laurie is CEO of Aligned at Work® in Scottsdale, AZ. Having spent 35+ years developing people in corporate environments, Laurie discovered ways to engage team members, build trust quickly, and align them with goals to create happy and high performing workplaces.

Laurie is the creator of the Aligned at Work® Model, which combines the Success Factors of Vocation, Relationships, Finances, Wellbeing, and Spirit into an integrated work/life model that brings humanity back to the workplace. She identified these factors in the thousands of leaders and team members with whom she worked as a leadership and organization development expert in the field of banking and finance. Her book, Aligned Workplaces: Integrating Life and Work - A Practical Guide for Leaders and Teams walks team members through the model and then provides helpful Team Leader Guides for running meetings about the 5 Success Factors.

Laurie spent the last half of her 35+ year corporate career working for some of the nation's largest investment and banking companies. Most recently, she was Vice President for Wells Fargo in Phoenix where she managed multiple teams of Learning and Development and Communications Professionals. Laurie is a former leadership development facilitator for Vanguard, the nation's largest mutual fund company.

Chapter Twelve

Laurie has an MS in Organizational Development and Leadership from Philadelphia College of Osteopathic Medicine, and a BS in Organizational Leadership from Eastern University in PA. She is a Professional Certified Coach and Master Practitioner for the Energy Leadership Index®, an assessment tool that measures types of energy and thought and how it shows up in people's lives, work, and relationships. She uses the Myers Briggs Type Indicator® (MBTI) and Everything DiSC® to increase leaders' self-awareness and diagnose team interactions. Her work with leaders and teams is based on the Drexler Sibbet Team Performance Model® and 5 Behaviors of a Cohesive Team™.

She is a member of the National Association of Women Business Owners (NAWBO), ELLEVATE Network, the International Coach Federation, the National Speakers Association, and the Arizona Organization Development Network. She volunteers with Hope's Crossing in Phoenix, a non-profit designed to help women who have been incarcerated, addicted, or headed down an unhealthy and unsafe track, to become healthy and whole.

Connect with Laurie:

Phone: (602) 888-0975
Email: laurie@alignedatwork.com
Website: www.AlignedAtWork.com
LinkedIn: Laurie Battaglia
Twitter: @alignedatwork
Facebook: @alignedatwork

Is Your Life and Work Slowly Killing You or Is It Feeding Your Soul?

Laurie Battaglia

"When was the last time you were happy to get in the car and go to work in the morning?" asked a friend of mine. This question caused me to sit back and think.

"Ten years ago," I said. And the die was cast. I had to leave that job. It took a while to get the pieces in place, but it was the best career move I ever made.

It wasn't easy. I had poured my heart and soul into that company and into the work I did there. It was great for the first three years. But I stayed nearly 13 years, and it wasn't that great at the end. I had run into a truly toxic boss, one who thought he knew all the answers for everyone. My sense of independence and autonomy, two of my biggest values, took a real hit. I like to say that my Guides and Angels made it so tough to stay there that I had to leave.

Ultimately, I moved from the "worst boss ever" to the "best boss ever." The place where I landed soothed my weary soul, rebuilt my confidence, and gave me a landing spot until I could launch my own business, Aligned at Work®.

My best boss understood me, and she understood what was important to me. She took time to talk with me, knew what made me tick, and gave me the freedom to do what I did well. I felt the greater purpose of what I was doing, and so did she. I hated to leave her. I wished I'd found her earlier and resolved

Chapter Twelve

to give back to her and the organization the value of what she gave to me.

Perhaps you've been there, too. Sometimes jobs or bosses are the "worst ever". They just aren't right for you. And that's okay because there are lots of organizations and leaders to choose from.

WHAT'S THE IMPACT TO YOUR LIFE?

As women entered the workforce in greater numbers in the late 1970s and early 80s, it was a man's world at work. People were expected to keep their home-life and their work-life separate. No pictures of family (unless you were the CEO who often displayed his family pictures proudly in his office). No personalized workspaces. No mention of children or things outside of work. None of the women in my office had children, so my 4-year-old was not talked about much unless he had an illness that prevented me from getting to work. And that meant a day off without pay in my bank teller job.

Fast forward to today. Both women and men bring all of work and life to the office and back home again. Technology makes it easy to check in at work while we're at home. We read emails while on vacation, never really disconnecting from work even during downtime. And our kids, partners, spouses and friends text us all day long at work. Work and life combine every day, all day.

DO THE MATH

Something that helped me put things into perspective about how much time and energy I spent working was the concept of "Do the Math".

Many of us talk about how important our family or our faith is, but when we sit down and calculate where we spend our time, work tends to be the clear winner in hours spent.

As a leader in organizations, my work time was often 45 to 50 hours per week. For 20 years of my life, I had at least a one

CHAPTER TWELVE

hour commute each way to work. With bad weather in the east coast, it was often 75 to 90 minutes each way. That's 2-3 hours of commute time in clogged highways, back roads, and bad drivers.

My day looked like this:
Up at 6 a.m., shower, dress, and prepare breakfast to eat in the car. Drive one hour to work arriving by 8 a.m., work until 5 p.m. taking an hour for lunch for sanity purposes. Commute another hour home, arriving around 6 p.m., make and eat dinner, watch some TV, get back online for work from 9 to 11 p.m., fall into bed, get back up at 6 a.m. and do it again.

Do you see any time for fun in there? For enjoying family or friends? For entertainment? Me neither. And don't get me started on weekend time. If you have a family, your weekends are not your own.

What does the math look like for you?

How many hours do you work each week? What's your commute time? How much time do you spend thinking about or worrying about work? I encourage you to do the math.

You have 168 hours per week to live, work, enjoy your family and friends and do whatever else you do. Most of us feel that the relationships in our lives outweigh our work concerning importance. And yet, we spend more time working than we do in most other categories of our lives.

It's crucial that you love your work, that it brings you joy, and that it feeds your soul. Stop doing work that sucks the life and soul right out of you! There are choices to make. Sometimes it's about long-term solutions, like education or relocation. The choices aren't always easy, but they give you options that you won't have without them.

BECOMING ALIGNED AT WORK® AND ALIGNED IN LIFE

Over many years of training and working with leaders, and being one myself, when you ask them about work/life balance, or work/life integration, as I call it, I realized that people have

Laurie Battaglia

these four things in common:

- They long for work that satisfies them.
- They'd like the work to support a larger cause.
- They want to have time to spend with family and friends, to travel, and to do other things that they want to do.
- They want to be authentic and do things that feed their souls.

With that in mind, a number of years ago I experienced a "Divine Download" as one of my friends calls it. On a long drive through the desert from California to Arizona, I created the Aligned at Work® Model. I realized that if these five areas of your life are synced up, you feel aligned and life and work are integrated as you choose them to be. Each of us has a different balance of the five categories.

In corporate terms, it's a great model for diverse teams. It helps people to feel included and fosters a sense of belonging. In personal terms, it's a great way to see where you are in alignment and where you aren't.

Vocation: Your work energizes you and fits your personal strengths. You share values with the company and fit the culture. Your works serves you and others.

Relationships: You form healthy relationships within yourself and with others, having a support system in place and serving as one for others.

Finances: You understand your relationship/mindset with money and understand basic financial concepts. You have your finances in order.

Wellbeing: Wellbeing is the state of being happy, healthy, and successful. You can define Wellbeing for you and understand where your definitions originate.

Spirit: Your Spirit is the authentic you. You know yourself. You see the connectedness in all things and believe in something larger than yourself.

CHAPTER TWELVE

Here's what the Aligned at Work® Model looks like.

Rate Yourself on the Aligned at Work® Success Factors

When you look at the categories of the model, how would you rate each one for you in your current work and life situation? If you had to rate yourself right now on a scale of 1 to 5, with 5 being "I've got it all together" and 1 being "Someone help me please!", where would you fall?

Next rate your workplace. On a scale of 1 to 5, with 5 being "Wow, my workplace and leaders really support me in this Success Factor" and 1 being "There is no human connection in this Success Factor and no support for this where I work", where does your workplace fall?

Success Factor	Personal Rating	Workplace Rating
Vocation	_____	_____
Relationships	_____	_____
Finances	_____	_____
Wellbeing	_____	_____
Spirit	_____	_____

Our lives and our work often shift and change. We may rate ourselves high one day and not so high the next. Bad bosses might transfer or leave the company, and suddenly things will start to look up.

Let's assume that like most people, you might have some Success Factors that are looking good and some others that aren't. What steps can you take to be more Aligned?

Laurie Battaglia

TEN TIPS FOR BEING ALIGNED AT WORK®, ALIGNED FOR LIFE

Vocation

1. Does your job match your personal values? Are you aligned with what your company stands for? Do online research on your company and do some research in person. Does what they say they stand for match the reality of what goes on day to day? If not, look for companies that match what you value. Do your homework before accepting a job.

2. Are you energized by the work you do, or do you go home exhausted every day? Do you know what kind of work you love best? Keep track over the next week or two. Write down what you are doing when you feel great and time passes quickly, and write down what you are doing when you are drained mentally, emotionally, or physically. How can you increase what you love and decrease what you dislike? Accomplish that, and you'll feel aligned!

Relationships

3. Who are the people who care about you? Do you have a support system in place around you? If not, begin slowly by connecting or networking with those around you—at work and in your community. Ask someone to go out for coffee. See if you can find things in common. Ask another person. Keep on doing this until you become aligned with someone who you enjoy spending your time with. Slowly, you'll build a community.

4. Rate the quality of the relationships you have with the people you spend the most time with. Are they positive, helpful and understanding? Are they dysfunctional? What role do you play in that? If you always find yourself in negative relationships, ask why that is. Are you allowing or settling for pessimistic relationships? In what other parts of your life does that show up? Align with positive people.

CHAPTER TWELVE

Financial

5. Does your job pay your bills and other things you want in your life? What is standing in the way of higher pay? Sometimes it's education, and sometimes it's our mindset. Some things take longer to achieve, like a degree or certification. Start now. Eventually you'll have it, and you'll be older anyway, with or without it! Other things can require help from experts, like changing your mindset. All things are achievable!

6. Do you understand basic budgeting and investing? Do you know how to prepare for large expenditures, like college and retirement? Saving small amounts from each paycheck adds up quicker than you think, thanks to the power of compounding interest. Take courses or hire a financial planner to help you understand your money and your goals. And here's a very simple piece of advice: If you don't understand the investment that is being recommended, don't invest in it. It's important to know where you stand. Now that's power!

Wellbeing

7. Happiness comes from within. How much of your happiness is dependent on forces or people outside of yourself? Begin by deciding that you ARE happy and take steps to make it so. How can you find time to align with yourself? Make time.

8. What is your definition of success? Do you know what you are striving for in your life, career, and relationships? Start by defining success in writing. Then figure out whether that definition is one you created yourself or adopted from listening to others. What do you want to be or achieve in your lifetime? Get started today.

Spirit

9. Who are you really – at the core? Define it. Now determine a way to take your authentic self to work, into your home and personal life and into your relationships. Do you feel like you need to leave your

soul at the door? What is it costing you? Journal until you know for sure.

10. We are all connected, and so are all the parts of our life and work. Find positive ways to live the connection between you and others. Lend someone a hand by volunteering. Align yourself with good, and the rewards will come back to you.

As you walk the path to Alignment, know that you have the power to make the changes you need in your life and work. When times are tough, they serve to let us know what's not working. Take heed of what your mind, body, and spirit are letting you know. Shifting even one thing today can have massive ripple effects in our personal history.

What would your life be like if all five Success Factors were in Alignment? Can you imagine?

Now go out and make it happen!

And remember this …

"Your work is going to fill a large part of your life, and the only way to be truly satisfied is to do what you believe is great work. And the only way to do great work is to love what you do. If you haven't found it yet, keep looking. Don't settle. As with all matters of the heart, you'll know when you find it."
~Steve Jobs

LEARN ABOUT
Joy
BRETZ- SHERRILL

Joy Bretz-Sherrill helps stressed-out professionals reclaim their time, well-being, finances and peace of mind.

In 2016, Joy went on a quest for a better life. She walked away from a 20+ year corporate career in financial management and went back to school to earn certifications in yoga and holistic nutrition.

From marrying young to raising a special needs child, divorce, financial hardships and health issues, Joy understands that the road isn't always easy. But that doesn't mean you can't Leave with Ease.

Joy's signature program - Leave with Ease - helps professionals create a professional exit strategy to create the work-life experience they desire. She can help you create a personalized roadmap to make the transition as smooth as possible while providing the accountability to keep you focused on your goals.

Connect with Joy Bretz-Sherrill:
Website: njoymindbodyandsoul.com
Facebook: @njoymindbodyandsoul
Instagram: @njoybnfit
LinkedIn: linkedin.com/company/njoybnfit

Chapter Thirteen

Is the Stress Really Worth It?

Joy Bretz-Sherrill

Have you ever asked yourself, "Is this all that there is to life?"

I remember asking myself that question, thinking, "If this is it, I'm not happy!" Working hard, being in debt and having no life is no way to live, but that's exactly what I was doing. My life belonged to everyone else but me.

Do you feel like work is getting in the way of the life you want? I'm not talking about lying on the beach sipping fruity drinks all day. I'm talking about critical factors like feeling a sense of purpose or spending time with your children and significant others.

A workplace survey conducted by Paychex Payroll Services in 2017 revealed that 81% of respondents wish they could spend more time with their kids. Thirty-one percent said that working overtime bothers their significant other or family.

I remember feeling like I was neglecting my family as I slaved away until 1 a.m. on a report my boss needed for a morning meeting only to have the meeting cancelled. To add insult to injury, they ended up not even needing the report at all because they decided to "go in a different direction."

From having unrealistic deadlines to dealing with difficult colleagues, work-related stress has become a documented occupational hazard.

Chapter Thirteen

WHAT IS WORK-RELATED STRESS?

Work-related stress is defined by Ireland's state-sponsored Health and Safety Authority as "stress caused or made worse by work when people perceive the work environment in a way that his or her reaction involves feelings of an inability to cope." It may be caused by real or perceived pressures, deadlines, threats or anxieties within the work environment. The World Health Organization even references work-related stress as an occupational health topic with negative organizational impact.

It's normal to deal with pressure related to our work from time to time. But what do you do if you reach a point where the paycheck and benefits no longer justify the physical and emotional toll? What if it's time to get out?

Freedom is possible. Here are three steps to get you started down the path.

STEP #1: FOLLOW YOUR J.O.Y.

The first step to freedom is to follow your J.O.Y.: Journey of You. The J.O.Y. is about understanding who you are and making changes that center and ground you to make decisions that will benefit you and your family's future. This is a process of internal change to shift your mindset so that you understand the power that you have within. With that power, you can create the life you deserve!

If you could do anything in the world related to the type of work-life experience you want, what would it be and why? Have you ever taken the time to think about it?

Finding my J.O.Y. took so long because I was living the life I was told I should live, not the life I wanted to live. Following the rules, doing the "right" thing and listening to everyone else but myself was the story of my life. All the while, I didn't feel smart enough and was afraid that people wouldn't like me. I was always thinking, "Am I making the right decisions? Did I make them mad?"

CHAPTER THIRTEEN

Those were the questions that plagued my thoughts. I was unsure of who I was and the contributions I was to give to this life. I realize now that the doubts, second guessing and lack of confidence delayed me from my J.O.Y. The process of knowing who I am and what I want out of this life began when I looked outside that window and asked the question, "Is this all that there is in this life?" It was that day that I went searching for more.

Many of us followed the rules given by our parents. Go to school, get good grades, go to college, get a good job, get married, have a family, be successful, and live a happy life. But along the way, challenges can get in the way of living "the dream".

Perhaps the most important question to ask yourself is if the dream you're pursuing is your dream or one that was unknowingly imposed upon you? What would it look like to live your dream?

What would it look like to take back your life and live on your own terms?

The Journey of You is about understanding who you are and not being ashamed or afraid to express that to the world – even if it doesn't fit its narrative of what success looks like.

Can you imagine what the people around me thought when I told them I was quitting my job as a corporate treasurer to be a yoga instructor? I had people tell me that I was crazy. They would ask me, "How could you give up such a great job and financial security to be a yoga teacher? They don't make a lot of money." And you see, that's just it. It wasn't about the money at that point in my life. I walked away because the stress was killing my spirit. My immune system was being compromised and I needed to tend to me. It was either stay at that job that was practically killing me, my time and my well-being or

Joy Bretz-Sherrill

choose me, my health and make a choice to be free. Having a healthy financial landscape gave me the opportunity to leave with ease so I could build a life for me and my family on my terms.

STEP #2: FOCUS ON YOUR HEALTH

We hold so much stress and tension in our bodies from emotions and from physical stresses like sitting in a chair for hours on end, typing on a laptop and carrying excess weight.

I knew I had to do something when being at my job started to make me sick…literally. I was experiencing brain fog, adrenal fatigue, bouts of insomnia, minimal sleep, hair loss and weight gain. Following a visit to my naturopathic doctor, I was diagnosed with having hypothyroidism. I had no idea what that was, but I knew I had to fix it. I asked my doctor if I could do my research first before I allowed him to put me on any medication; he agreed. I became so engrossed in finding long-term solutions for myself that I knew I had to help others, too.

I never realized how much stress I internalized until I stepped on a yoga mat. The practice of yoga not only helped me manage my stress, but it also helped me realize my purpose. When I made the decision to walk away from my job, it wasn't a difficult decision. I knew I was divinely led to take the leap of my life, and I was filled with faith. I trusted that God and the Universe were guiding me.

After 90 days of educating myself, learning my body and taking care of me, I was able to balance my hormones, regulate my thyroid and bring myself back in alignment without medication. If you want to experience true success, your health must be a priority. *Period*. Without your health, you can't work towards anything else because you are in survival mode. Being aligned in mind, body and spirit is critical to your overall well-being.

I recently experienced a serious health issue where my quick recovery was deemed a "medical miracle" by health care professionals. I know that my lifestyle practices played a big role in how fast I was able to bounce back.

CHAPTER THIRTEEN

I practice yoga and meditate daily using the strength of the breath to manage my responses to emotional situations. Daily yoga practice has numerous well-documented benefits, including boosting the immune system, easing migraines, increasing flexibility, relieving stress, improving digestion and more.

Yoga helped me improve my mental, physical and emotional existence. It transformed my lifestyle, so I now respond to life instead of reacting to it. I know how to manage external triggers so that they do not draw me into a negative experience. But if they do, I know how to reset my internal compass and redirect myself back to center.

Let's be honest, it can be a daily challenge to not react to certain people, places or things. By having the tools to help you transition through the experience, you can separate your feelings from the actions.

STEP #3: FREE YOUR FINANCES

The primary reason people stay in jobs or careers that no longer serve them is because they can't afford not to. If you lost your job tomorrow, how long could you and your family survive? What does your current financial landscape look like? Are you living beyond your means to keep up appearances or are you being practical and future focused?

These are some very serious questions you need to be asking yourself because there's no such thing as job security. I created a program called Leave with Ease that helps people create a practical financial plan to transition to the work-life experience they desire. If you're the primary breadwinner in your household, waking up tomorrow and deciding to quit your job without having preparations in place is not an advisable strategy.

Even if your financial picture isn't ideal today, it doesn't have to stay that way. Remember, you have the power within to create the life you deserve. You don't have to be a victim, chained to a

Joy Bretz-Sherrill

job you hate or answering to a boss who doesn't respect you. I was able to walk away from my job and maintain the same lifestyle I had as a corporate employee. If I can do it, you can too.

In my first marriage, we were constantly looking for better paying jobs to pay off debt. We lived our entire marriage in debt. During three separate occasions, we racked up debt and paid it off, but we never learned the lessons along the way. The daily burden of wondering where the money was going to come from to pay for the lifestyle we created was a lot to bear for both of us. It was during that fourth and final time of being in debt that I said no more! I was in my final year of grad school, and I realized that if I wanted life to be different for me and my children, I had to change. It was that day I changed my view of my financial landscape and never looked back.

The strategies, techniques and tools I learned would help me skyrocket my career, increase my financial wealth and make my money work for me instead of me working for my money. And it was the steps during those years that afforded me the opportunity to step out of that corporate life, live life on my own terms and help prepare and teach others how to do the same.

Between the gig economy and low barriers to entry for entrepreneurship, everyday people are finding ways to make a living doing what they love. If you do the work now, you can Leave with Ease!

If you're still asking yourself, "Is working hard, being in debt and having no life all there is?", the answer is "no". But a

> **You have the power to create the life you want, even if it feels like your bank account says otherwise.**

CHAPTER THIRTEEN

different life will require you to make different choices.

You may not be able to turn in your letter of resignation tomorrow, so focusing on your health and effectively managing stress through practices like meditation and yoga can help to keep you from reaching your breaking point until you can transition.

Making significant lifestyle changes can be challenging to make on your own. That's why I created the Leave with Ease program. **Leave with Ease** teaches you how to shift your mindset so you can prepare to make the changes needed to live life on your terms. You'll also learn the tools and techniques to manage your finances instead of letting your finances manage you.

Most of all, you'll build new opportunities for your future that you could not see when your life, time, money and well-being were managed by others.

Leave with Ease is your opportunity to finally say, "I choose me!" Investing in you is the best and most powerful thing you could ever do. You are saying "yes" to a generational shift in your bloodline. It all starts with you.

For a free webinar to help you get started, visit our website at *www.leavewithease.com.*

Joy Bretz-Sherrill

LEARN ABOUT
BRENDA MARIAH CUNNINGHAM

Brenda Cunningham is the CEO of Push Career Management. Her company provides professional resumes, LinkedIn profiles, job search and interview coaching that has supported hundreds of emerging leaders in landing their dream jobs and climbing the corporate ladder. In addition to working with individuals, Brenda's company provides outplacement services for small to medium-sized companies who need to reduce their workforce.

Brenda is on a mission to provide practical, career-advancing resources to super smart professionals. She is the author of Crush the Pink Slip: Get Back to Work in 60 Days, host of the podcast, The Day Before Monday, and she frequently speaks on career-related topics.

Recognized as a leader in the industry, Brenda is president of the Resume Writers' Council of Arizona. She is a Certified Professional Resume Writer (CPRW), Certified Job Search Strategist (CJSS) and Credentialed Career Manager (CCM).

Contact Brenda Mariah Cunningham:
Website: PushCareerManagement.com
LinkedIn: Brenda M. Cunningham
Facebook: @PushCareers

Chapter Fourteen

How to Fire-Proof Your Career

Brenda Mariah Cunningham

If you work in corporate America, you must read this chapter.

As you have probably figured out by now, the private sector is not the safe haven of job security that it once used to be. Even so, layoffs at some companies shocked us all. In the media industry, we've watched newsrooms dwindle to bare minimum staffing levels while some outlets have folded completely. But who would've ever guessed a powerhouse brand like ESPN would be disrupted? Entire industries such as mining and telecommunications are disappearing, while brick-and-mortar retail operations are being shut out of the marketplace by the Amazon behemoth.

Nine years into my corporate career, I was a project manager and engineer for a global semiconductor manufacturing company. Even though the company had more than 10,000 employees, I still felt like I was making a major difference – not just another cog in the machine. My projects were saving hundreds of millions of dollars and ensuring business continuity for my company and our customers. Yet, that didn't matter. Although I was able to escape two earlier rounds of layoffs, when times got tough, it was my turn in the line of fire for downsizing.

Layoffs are real, and they are happening everyday. Layoffs are far too common for us to continue to feel like we are "safe" in the corporate world. The best defense we can bring to the

Chapter Fourteen

world of work is a good offense.

UNDERSTAND THAT YOU ARE REPLACEABLE

As awesome as you are at your job, when it comes down to the bottom line, you will be considered dispensable unless you can repeatedly prove your value to your employer. Here are three specific things you can do to demonstrate your contributions:

1. **Bring solutions, not complaints.** If there is ever a new process that you disagree with or an old process that's no longer effective, think through at least two alternatives to present before voicing your concerns or complaining to co-workers.

2. **Invest in yourself.** With training and development budgets slashed as the economy started taking dips and dives, the dollars that used to be available for you to attend conferences or pursue certifications are no longer there. Understand that it is your job to stay relevant, and if they won't invest in you, invest in yourself. Lifelong learning is not just a cute phrase that sounds good in school; it is a truth you must embrace if you are to become fire-proof.

3. **Know how you contribute and make sure the key decision makers know that you've crushed your metrics.** Of course, this starts with a clear line of sight to the powers that be. You must know who they are and more importantly, they must know you if you are to even get close to their radars. When it comes to decisions about promotions, salary increases, and who the MVPs are for the organization, they must know you and what major things you've done for them lately. This is easier said than done, so please take time to understand who the players are in your organization and in related divisions within your company. Knowing how well you're doing isn't just good for the sake of your job, it's also imperative for your annual resume update. How else will you be able to showcase how valuable you are on paper?

CHAPTER FOURTEEN

KNOW THE STATE OF YOUR INDUSTRY

I'm still shocked that the taxi cab industry didn't see their troubles coming sooner. Did they seriously not consider Uber a threat? Once Lyft came along, did cab drivers still not see the writing on the wall? It makes my head spin when the majority of people in affected industries miss such obvious indicators of change. Watching or listening to the news helps, but by the time they're talking about it, you're already in trouble. Subscribing to an industry journal or newsletter and attending relevant professional conferences will keep you up-to-date on current trends, opportunities and threats to your industry. You must wake up and pay attention if you want to keep yourself out of the painful pit of a layoff. Being proactive and knowing what's moving and shaking within your industry is no longer a nice-to-have, but a true necessity.

UNDERSTAND THE DIFFERENCE YOU MAKE

Equally important, make sure your company cares about those contributions. Just because you have a super fun and exciting project doesn't mean you're irreplaceable. It is your job to know if your company's leaders actually care about that work. If that project is not mission critical, you may be spending too many of your precious hours doing the wrong work. Doing work that isn't valued is almost certain to land you in that private office where you'll receive your pink slip.

TIME YOUR INTERNAL MOVES CAREFULLY

If you don't know the state of things and you move at an inopportune time, you may end up being a LIFO: Last in, first out. Do you have a good working knowledge of the budgetary cycles in your industry or company? This is just as important as knowing the functions of your job. When you are striving to keep yourself out of the line of fire, one thing that's often overlooked is timing. Has there been a recent leadership change? This typically shuffles things around to unrecognizable proportions. Do you see the writing on the wall or have rumors of layoffs been circulating around the water cooler? If so, ask yourself, "Is this really the best time to go after a new position internally?" Please learn from me that LIFO is a real thing and being strategic with your transitions should not be an afterthought.

Brenda Cunningham

KNOW PEOPLE OUTSIDE OF YOUR DEPARTMENT AND COMPANY

This is a biggie! It's easy to get so caught up in the minutiae of our jobs and daily tasks lists that we rarely, if ever, make time to meet other people in our industry. We walk around in our imaginary comfort bubbles assuming that our jobs are secure until we decide otherwise, and this is simply not the case.

What happens if your entire department is laid off and none of your former colleagues have a job they could pull you into? This happens more often than you might think and if everyone enters the job market at the same time, your competition pool just got deeper and more cutthroat because you're vying for positions with others that you know are amazing. But what if you knew other people outside the walls of your building? That puts you in a position to leverage those relationships to gain access to positions at their places of employment. This is not the same as using people; it's the byproduct of cultivating relationships.

Far too often, I see people wait until they need a new job and then rush to engage with people they haven't spoken to in years— frantically throwing together some semblance of a LinkedIn profile. How eager do you think those individuals will be to help you when they are only hearing from you because you need something from them? Not very.

BE PREPARED AND BECOME FIRE-PROOF

Here are a few steps to consider during your next performance review. If your company doesn't conduct formal appraisals, you can initiate this process on your own:

- It is essential that you start the dialogue with your immediate boss (and inform his/her boss) stating your intention to make the biggest possible difference for the company.

- Request or propose projects that are in line with the company's most urgent, revenue-impacting area. Recall that not everything will just be handed to you.

CHAPTER FOURTEEN

It's your job to keep tabs on what's important to your leadership. You need to know what's coming down the pipeline in your industry and what innovations can help to keep your company relevant.

- Once you've taken inventory of those things, now you've got something concrete to propose.
- Do such an excellent job that they can't deny you. Excellence is the key.

I truly believe that I went through a devastating layoff in my career so that you don't have to. Unless your company is closing its doors for good, there is no reason you have to be among the numbers receiving layoff notices.

Of course, following these strategies are not a guarantee because there are many factors that could influence a company's decision to downsize. However, embracing these methods certainly stack the odds in your favor.

God bless you as you continue to navigate the remainder of your career. If you need help navigating the waters, visit **PushCareerManagement.com**.

Brenda Cunningham

LEARN ABOUT
Dr. Nadia
BROWN

Dr. Nadia Brown is an authentic, bold champion for women business owners. She is the founder and CEO of The Doyenne Agency, Inc., a global sales and sales training company.

Through her workshops and intensives, she helps women break through the glass ceilings they encounter in business by helping them build profitable and sustainable businesses. When it comes to sales, women come to her timid and shaky about going after the money, but they leave her strategic, strong, emboldened and most importantly, paid.

Dr. Nadia helped clients generate over $1.3 million dollars in sales in 2018 and has been featured in publications such as Black Enterprise Magazine and the Huffington Post.

She is the author of Leading Like a Lady: How to Shatter Your Inner Glass Ceiling, Selling Like a Lady: Courage Diary and the forthcoming book How to Master Sales with Dignity, Class and Grace. She lives with her husband Toby in Phoenix, AZ.

Connect with Dr. Nadia Brown:
Website: TheDoyenneAgency.com
LinkedIn: Dr. Nadia Brown
Facebook: @TheDrNadia
YouTube: Doyenne Leadership

Chapter Fifteen

Ask for What You Desire

Dr. Nadia Brown

"I need to talk… like really talk," read the email from one of my good friends. I immediately typed back, "When are you available?"

When it took her too long to respond, I picked up the phone and called her. I needed to know that she was okay. Once we got on the phone, she shared the frustration that she had with herself for not negotiating her salary when she accepted her current job, and she was trying to rectify that.

"I'm underpaid. I know I deserve more. I'm kicking myself because I knew better. I should have negotiated."

Her frustration also caused her to take a look at her business. She has a side hustle that she wants to eventually grow to her full-time job. The problem is that she's not making enough money in her side hustle, either. You see, the problem of not asking for what she desires is also being carried over to her business. She's not charging the prices that she needs to charge in order to be able to leave her job, or even making the money she knows she deserves to make on her job.

Talk about a conundrum.

Can you relate?

I have so been there on both fronts; working in corporate and

Chapter Fifteen

in my business. I remember knowing in my head to negotiate my salary and I'd even done it successfully in the past, but for some reason when I received that job offer, I just jumped at the first number they threw at me. I did that even when I knew I was leaving at least $10,000 per year on the table. Can you say, "OUCH?!"

I also remember a time when I knew it was time to raise the rates in my business, but I ended up doing the same thing. When it came time to give the prospective clients a higher number, I froze and the words didn't come out of my mouth.

When I'd walk away from sales conversations, all I could think is, "Why can't I seem to charge more?" Or more importantly, "Why can't I seem to ask for what I desire?" I knew I should, but for some reason my actions weren't aligning with my inner knowing.

So what do you do? How do you overcome this? That was a question my girlfriend asked me.

"I need you to help me snap out of it!" she said.

She was really frustrated with herself for not doing the things that she knew she should have done and now she was facing the prospect of having to have this really uncomfortable conversation, asking for her salary to be adjusted.

I have a lot of conversations with mostly women entrepreneurs around the issue of undercharging for their services or really looking at what they want to earn in their businesses. Whether you are an employee or a business owner, you have to know how to ask for what you desire and what you feel you deserve, especially if you're a woman.

According to the Bureau of Labor Statistics, a woman employee earns just 83 cents for every dollar a man earns. The numbers are even worse for women entrepreneurs. According to this same study, a woman business owner earns just 80 cents for every dollar a man earns.

CHAPTER FIFTEEN

So how do you snap out of it? Here are seven keys to put into practice to start asking for what you desire:

1. **Practice self-compassion.** Just because your head knows what to do doesn't mean you'll automatically do it every time. When you don't, it's easy to fall into the cycle of beating yourself up. However, this is not productive. Letting go of the guilt and making a commitment to practice self-compassion is key. You won't always get it right, and that's okay. That's what makes you human.

2. **Get clear on what you desire.** I've had the opportunity to train hundreds of women over the years, and I cannot begin to tell you the number of times I've asked a woman about her vision and she wasn't sure of what she truly desired. It is so easy to get caught up in trying to live up to the desires and vision of someone else, but what is your vision? What do you desire? It's not just talking about how much money you want to make. Spend some time getting clear on your big vision, and from there you can develop the road map and strategy to get you there.

3. **Own your brilliance.** We are all equipped with unique gifts and talents, but many of us don't like to own them. No matter how many degrees, certifications, certificates, or years of experience we have, we still have this challenge. I don't know what it is, but those gremlins will start talking – the voices in your head who start to make you doubt yourself or compare yourself to someone else.

   Don't do that.

> **You won't always get it right, and that's okay. That's what makes you human.**

Own your greatness. Own your skills. Own your experience. Own your insight. Own your gifts. I mean truly own them and unapologetically acknowledge them. This is the key in asking for what you desire. If you continue to downplay and deny the powerful force that is in you, guess what? You start to believe the lie that you are not worthy of more or better. Then subconsciously you start to buy into the lie that maybe you really don't deserve what you truly desire.

4. **Define your next steps.** Now that you are clear on your big vision and your unique gifts, it's time to put together your plan of action. What do you need to do to get you there? Map out what you need to do, and also identify any resources you may need in order to complete that particular action successfully. Be sure to add dates for your different milestones.

5. **Take action.** Now that you have your plan, it is time to get to work. We like to talk about a lot of stuff, watch videos and read books, don't we? We do all of these

> ***Own all of your brilliance and your unique contribution to this world. Then refuse to apologize for being amazing.***

different things, but you won't see anything different until you take action. And I have to add this – baby steps count.

What you desire may feel too big. You may feel like asking for that big of a salary increase or making that big of a jump in your rates will never work. The truth is that "big" is relative. Don't allow the size of your goal intimidate or overwhelm you. Identify one thing you can do on a daily or weekly basis that will move you

CHAPTER FIFTEEN

closer to your goal. Then do it.

6. **Track your progress**. You have undoubtedly heard the saying, "What gets measured, gets done." Create a way to track your progress. It doesn't have to be overly complicated; it just needs to be something that you will actually do.

   When I first started tracking my numbers on a consistent basis, I simply created a simple Google spreadsheet. I initially shared it for accountability purposes, but you don't have to. Not only was it simple, but when I stuck to it, I began to see massive results in a short amount of time. Commit to doing an audit at least quarterly to see what's working, what could work better and how you may need to tweak your strategy for maximum effectiveness.

7. **Celebrate your wins** - Many times, we wait until the big goal is achieved before we celebrate. Some of us don't celebrate at all. Develop a celebration plan where you decide on ways to acknowledge the smaller milestones along the way. This is something that I developed when I was going through my doctoral program and implemented again last year as my team and I worked towards achieving our sales and revenue goals.

Not only does it feel good, but it is a total game changer. Some celebration ideas are happy dances, massages and bubble baths. You can buy yourself a gift or spend time with a friend. The list is endless! Get creative. Have fun. It doesn't matter what you do. The important part is that you celebrate yourself along the way.

Asking for what you desire is a skill. Think of it as a muscle that must be developed. Give yourself time. It won't happen overnight, but in time you will find that you have no problem asking for what you desire unapologetically and with no guilt.

To stay connected, visit **TheDoyenneAgency.com** and sign up to join our community where I share weekly Straight Talk About Sales videos along with other resources and insight.

Dr. Nadia Brown

LEARN ABOUT
Lawrence
RIDDICK

Lawrence Riddick is a renaissance man of marketing with vast experience spanning 18 years. The founding principal of The Riddick Agency, Lawrence has worked with renowned automotive brands under the General Motors umbrella in the areas of branding, experiential and content marketing. He is also a purveyor of marketing services for small businesses and has a high competency in design and strategic marketing initiatives.

Educated at Northwood University in Midland, Michigan, Lawrence resides in Jacksonville, Florida with his wife, Yubeka and daughter, Cherith. He is driven by indomitable spirit, legacy, family, and coffee.

Connect with Lawrence Riddick:
Website: RiddickAgency.com
Twitter: riddickpoint0
Instagram: riddickagency
LinkedIn: Lawrence Riddick

Chapter Sixteen

Why Social Media Is NOT a Marketing Strategy

Lawrence Riddick

What would happen if all social media channels disappeared tomorrow? Would you still be able to attract new customers or would your business flatline?

For the past decade, social media has been "the most popular girl at the party" when it comes to marketing. With nonstop emergence of new platforms promising to be the game changer for small businesses, I'm willing to wager you won't leave a business conference these days without hearing, "You need a social media strategy."

It's true. You need a plan of action to use social media, but it can't be the only thing you focus on when it comes to marketing.

THE BENEFITS OF SOCIAL MEDIA MARKETING
Just like there are trends in consumer purchasing, there are also trends in the way brands market to potential customers. Before social media, businesses were doing just fine reaching their audiences. However, social media has mitigated a mandatory expense of high cost media and eliminated the gatekeepers that kept you from the people you want to connect with. Social media currently offers you a low cost of entry to reach your customer base, and it is easier to quantify the return on investment (ROI) versus tactics in traditional media, where measurements can be more difficult to track.

Chapter Sixteen

Social media can provide a significant boost to the marketing mix when you have a solid content strategy. But what I have found is that many small businesses have diverted all of their marketing efforts into social media only. Maybe it's laziness. Maybe it's just riding the trend. But at the end of the day, putting all of your eggs in one basket is never wise.

Your customers are not one-dimensional. Most people won't make decisions based upon seeing something once on social media. They need to become familiar with a brand and see it across multiple channels in order for it to even register to them that you exist. Good brands brilliantly and systematically approach their consumers across multiple mediums to help bring them closer to a purchase.

Am I saying that your marketing strategy focused solely on using social media is wrong? No, but I am saying that your social media strategy is NOT a marketing strategy.

THINK BEYOND THE HASHTAG
Every business needs a comprehensive marketing strategy. What is that? An all-inclusive plan that defines your customer, value proposition and positioning combined with a communications plan that creatively distributes your message through a variety of channels. When you're thinking about those channels, don't just focus on social media. Think media! While traditional channels like print, radio and TV are not dominating attention as they did before, they still make up a formidable chunk of the marketing mix for brands that successfully reach their customers.

As a marketer approaching 20 years in the business, I have seen marketing evolve and shift. Marketing is such a broad and exhaustive discipline, and I do recognize that there are different philosophies and schools of thought when it comes to marketing. Some schools of thought last longer than others, but jumping on the wave of every short-lived craze can dilute your brand in the eyes of your consumer.

It is essential that you get advice from someone who studies

CHAPTER SIXTEEN

and understands the discipline of marketing and consumer behavior – not just a one-trick pony who read a couple of articles about the latest social media tool. I am a student of the game of marketing, so rest easy.

I have consulted brands to ride trends early for maximum return, but more importantly, to only stay married to their brand and their consumer. Tactics and trends fade, but the consumers will always be 'king'. Think of marketing as a marathon, not a

> **Jumping on the wave of every short-lived craze can dilute your brand in the eyes of your consumer.**

sprint. You want your consumer to trust that your brand will hold its promise. They need to believe that your brand will be what it says it is, no matter what vehicle you use to reach them.

7 BE'S OF MARKETING

So you may ask, how do I stay relevant with my marketing approach, without killing my brand? I have seven tips that will help you get out of the weeds of the chasing the latest marketing trends and into building a sustainable marketing strategy to grow your business. I call it the 7 Be's of Marketing:

1. **Be Strategic** - Winging it with your marketing can waste a lot of time and money. It can also confuse your customers. Don't just jump in with a series of tactics – develop a strategy. A solid marketing strategy combines your core values with your value proposition to formulate your advantage. This advantage will help you define your branding and craft your plan to reach new customers and keep your existing loyal customers.

2. **Be Results-Oriented** - Remember, it's a marathon, not a sprint. As you run your race, keep your ears open and listen to the marketplace – especially your customers. They communicate with their wallets, with positive and

negative feedback, and with their silence. Prioritize what you hear from them and make adjustments as needed.

Your campaign may be clever, but is it delivering results? It's critical to routinely evaluate the performance of your programs. Take a look at your business and ask questions like:

- Are you collecting feedback or customer data?
- What is the data telling you?
- What is the perception of your brand in the marketplace?
- What are the best mediums to reach your audience?
- What is the Return on Investment (ROI) for your spending?

While working for a large agency, it always baffled me when my clients wanted us to set the bar for their business and marketing goals. Your marketing goals should align with your business goals. If you want to increase sales by 25% in the 4th quarter, what you do in marketing should be strictly aligned with your business goals. If someone else is driving your marketing goals, they are driving your business.

There is nothing wrong with having consultants and agencies help you develop and execute plans to achieve your business goals faster, but they should not be setting your goals. Your goals must be measurable and driven by YOU.

3. **Be Consistent** - Building a plan and walking that plan out is tough if you are not committed to it. Millions of people set New Year's resolutions that don't make it out of the month of January. Don't do this with your marketing goals. No judgment here because I know how challenging it can be, and I have struggled myself.

If you're running a marathon for the first time,

CHAPTER SIXTEEN

consistent training is critical to successfully complete the race. As you train, you'll find out what things work well for you and what don't, like what shoes to wear, foods to eat and how much to hydrate as your distances increase. If you're inconsistent with your efforts, it will be challenging to get an accurate gauge on what's working or not. The same is true when it comes to your marketing efforts. When you sink your teeth in and commit to your marketing plan, you can gather so much information about your customers that will help you understand their behaviors. This will show you how to reach them more effectively.

Take an honest look in the mirror and ask yourself, "How bad do I really want to succeed?" Remember why your goals are important to you and use that as fuel to stay committed to your marketing activities.

4. **Be Adaptable** - When Netflix DVD service came on the scene, Blockbuster bet the future of their business on the notion that no one would want to wait days to get their movies. Because they were so set on where customer behavior was instead of where it was going, Blockbuster's brick and mortar business went belly up.

   Markets shift, consumer behavior evolves, and new players come on the scene that may require you to adapt. It may be a minor tweak or perhaps you need to pivot in an entirely different direction. It's okay to be wrong. It's not okay to be wrong, know you're wrong, and still refuse to make the adjustments.

5. **Be Resilient** - There are no absolutes in business. You will launch efforts and even make investments that don't pan out. When it comes to your marketing, if the data shows you that your efforts aren't delivering the results you desire, don't be so married to your plan that you're unwilling to try a new approach. Don't beat yourself up; just lace your shoes up and get back in the race.

6. **Be Patient** - Now there is a flipside to this, and that is endurance. I see some marketers lose patience with

Lawrence Riddick

> **Remember why your goals are important to you and use that as fuel to stay committed to your marketing activities.**

their plan without giving it time to deliver. Maybe you don't see enough leads or your market research told you that your customer wanted a particular product, but it's not selling through the roof as you expected. When you invest time and money into your marketing efforts but your ROI is non-existent, your natural urge may be to quit. You need patience to endure the process.

Before you jump ship, ask yourself, "Have I set realistic expectations around the timeline and projected results?" Every launch isn't going to be an overnight success, but that doesn't mean it won't be effective long-term. Continue to watch the data and listen to your customers.

Just like a tree, a new marketing program needs time to take root before you'll see the growth on the surface. If you keep pulling up the seeds and planting new ones before they mature, you'll never experience the growth you desire for your business.

7. **Be Resourceful** - If you are the key decision maker in the business, you should always drive your marketing strategy and goals. It is too close to the vitality of your business not to have a hand on the direction of your marketing. However, if you're looking to grow your business, you can't wear all of the hats alone.

When it comes to your marketing, where are the gaps? Do you need a consultant to help you fine-tune your social media content plan or a good creative agency to help develop visuals to bring the essence of your

CHAPTER SIXTEEN

brand to light? Some businesses need help developing the strategy but have the ability to follow the plan. Others need extra hands to carry out the day-to-day execution of the strategy.

As you look at your business strategy and where you want to grow, identify what you need most on the marketing side and hire a freelancer or agency to help you get there. You may think you can't afford to hire help, but the real question is if you can afford not to. No matter how focused you are, there are still only 24 hours in a day. Getting the right support at the right stage of your business almost always pays for itself.

When it comes to your marketing strategy, think of it as a delicious four-course meal. Just as each of the elements complement the other to provide an enjoyable dining experience, each element of the marketing mix complements the other to deliver results in your business. While social media can give your business a voice and an advantage in the digital world, it should not be the only thing on the plate. If you want to grow your business, effective marketing is essential.

Start with SMART business goals. Listen to your customers. Be consistent and patient, and evaluate the performance of your marketing program. When you follow these steps, you will have a recipe for long-term success!

If you feel stuck or overwhelmed, I can help. Email me at *discover@riddickagency.com* and I will respond personally.

Lawrence Riddick

LEARN ABOUT
ISHA COGBORN

Whether she's hosting satellite broadcasts with Oscar-winning actress Hilary Swank, giving career advice in magazines like Ebony and Cosmo, or landing in the top three percent of finalists for a show on the Oprah Winfrey Network, Isha's mission is to help people build the careers of their dreams.

She is als is the founder of Epiphany Institute – a personal development firm that helps people connect their purpose and passion to their profession. She specializes in personal brand building for purpose-driven authors, coaches, consultants and subject-matter experts.

Isha is the host of the podcast, On Purpose with Isha Cogborn and founder of the Platform for Purpose Initiative to amplify the voices of people who want to make a bigger impact in the world. She's the author of personal branding primer, 5 Rules to Win Being You, and the force behind the book, On Purpose: Practical Strategies to Live Your Best Life.

When you work with Isha, it's like hiring three experts in one – a certified life and corporate coach, business strategist and a seasoned PR pro with who served as a global communications and branding manager for one of the world's largest corporations.

Tried by fire, Isha operates with resilience birthed from being a teenage mother on welfare, corporate layoffs and a bout

Chapter Seventeen

of homelessness after a failed business venture. Determined to find purpose in her struggles, Isha founded Startup Life Support in 2017 to help entrepreneurs overcome the fear, frustration and isolation of starting a business.

Isha earned a degree in Broadcast and Cinematic Arts from Central Michigan University. She's a member of Alpha Kappa Alpha Sorority, Inc. and a volunteer with Kauffman Foundation's 1 Million Cups initiative.

Connect with Isha Cogborn

Website: EpiphanyInstitute.com
Podcast: OnPurposePodcast.com
Facebook: @coachisha
LinkedIn: Isha Cogborn
Email: Isha@EpiphanyInstitute.com

Platform for Purpose: How to Grow Your Audience and Your Impact

Isha Cogborn

Since I was 14 years old, I knew that I wanted to share information that would change people's lives and inspire them to be better versions of themselves. I wanted to have a platform for people who were doing good in the world so that their impact could be even greater.

Charting a career today with that mission might seem like a no-brainer thanks to social media, self-publishing and the ability to create an internationally-known personal brand with your mobile phone. But back then, the only path that seemed to make sense was becoming a journalist.

After earning a degree in broadcast journalism, I discovered a startling fact: I hated news. Maybe hate is a strong word. And I didn't dislike all news, just the depressing stuff. I knew my sensitive spirit couldn't handle covering tragedy and mayhem day in and day out. Instead, I ended up in corporate communications where I actually got an opportunity to host and produce a TV show and global broadcasts for a chemical company. Imagine that! But the higher I ascended on the corporate ladder, the further away I got from the work I loved.

After getting laid off in 2009, I founded Epiphany Institute, a professional development company that helps people connect their purpose and passions with their profession. I discovered that new options existed to create the profession I dreamed about as a teenager. When I realized I could forge a path not

Chapter Seventeen

limited to the bullet points of a corporate job description, I wanted to shout it from the mountaintops so everyone would know they had options, too!

I also discovered that I could now reach people without the gatekeepers of traditional media. In the years to come, I launched a blog, started my own podcast and self-published books (including the one you're reading). Not once did I ask for anyone's permission or jump through hoops to prove that I was worthy of sharing my message.

But as the tools get easier to use and more people jump into the fray, it's becoming harder to capture meaningful attention. Social media platforms like Facebook, Instagram and LinkedIn use ever-changing algorithms to serve up the most popular content to users. The more people who engage with your content, the more it shows up in timelines and newsfeeds. Content creators who used to enjoy major traction are now relying on sponsored posts to hit the same numbers.

RISE OF THE INFLUENCERS

The early 2000's ushered in a wave of celebrities like Paris Hilton and Kim Kardashian who were both lauded and loathed as being "famous for nothing." From reality shows to clothing lines, these personalities learned how to monetize their magnetism.

Today, this strategy isn't limited to hotel heiresses and the Hollywood elite. Regular people just like you are building personal brands that attract the attention of companies looking to cut through the noise and humanize their brands. While the focus used to be on social media users with huge followings, brands are now recognizing that quantity doesn't always mean quality when it comes to a loyal audience. An entire industry has emerged to match the right influencers with the right brands.

Influencers are 'word of mouth marketing on steroids' because they already have a following who trust their opinions. It's important to note that these tribes aren't always built because

CHAPTER SEVENTEEN

the influencer is the most knowledgeable source available but often because their personality, values or experiences create a connection with their audience.

WHY DOES THIS MATTER TO YOU?

Whether you're looking to attract brands and sponsors or just want to deliver your message more meaningfully, simply putting information out there and hoping people pay attention won't cut it anymore. You have to infuse *you* into your message.

Why are there hundreds of books on a single topic available on Amazon? Why has cable news viewership eclipsed local ratings? Because people crave connection, not just information. They're looking for someone who gets them.

We all have the ability to present a different take on a topic based on who we are, our life experiences and the lens through which we see the world. However, too many of us have pushed our views and personality down to our toes because someone told us we were too quirky, not polished enough or that our opinions were too polarizing.

There are people who will never like you, no matter how hard you work to win them over. Instead of focusing on them, what if you found the people who will love you just the way you are? I'm not saying you shouldn't focus on improving the way you deliver a message, but that's not the same as force-fitting yourself into someone else's box. What makes you different from other people who do what you do may be the very thing that attracts your tribe. It's the essence of your personal brand.

WHAT IS PERSONAL BRANDING?

Many oversimplify branding as logos or color schemes associated with a product or business. While visual elements may represent the brand, it goes much deeper. Here's my favorite definition of branding:

"Branding is the recognition of a personal connection that forms in the hearts and minds of customers and key audiences through their accumulated experience at every point of contact."

Although difficult to measure in dollars and cents, branding is a form of currency. A strong, positive brand fosters loyalty that keeps customers from jumping ship for competitors. Because a brand is built through accumulated experiences over time, customers are also more forgiving of errors if the bulk of their experiences have been positive.

I first became acquainted with the term "personal branding" after reading a 1997 article by Tom Peters in Fast Company magazine. Although I may not have had the terminology to explain it, I understood from an early age that I had some control over the narrative that formed in people's heads when they interacted with me. From the clothes I wore to the

> **"Branding is the recognition of a personal connection that forms in the hearts and minds of customers and key audiences through their accumulated experience at every point of contact."**

extracurricular clubs I joined, I made choices that aligned with the way I wanted people to see me. When I landed a co-op job at a bank at the age of 16, I wore business suits to school. People in other departments thought I was a full-time salaried employee!

Everything you do (or don't do) either strengthens or diminishes your personal brand. There was a consultant I had been watching on social media with thoughts of signing up for one of her programs. When I saw her go on a tirade about a customer, I decided to go another route. I'm sure she was just having a bad day and let her frustration get the best of her, but I hadn't had enough positive experiences with her yet to keep it from negatively impacting my opinion of her. None of us are perfect, but being deliberate about the way we show up in the

CHAPTER SEVENTEEN

world increases our chances of attracting and retaining the right audience. In case you think I'm contradicting myself from earlier in the chapter, please understand that it's not about trying to make everyone happy. It's about not unintentionally driving away the people we want to work with.

THE POWER OF A PLATFORM

Social media gives you the opportunity to communicate more broadly than ever before, but sharing your opinion doesn't mean you have a platform. At any time, you can be put into "Facebook jail" if you do something that breaks their rules because it's not YOUR platform. You are a user on THEIR platform. Building a platform means creating vehicles that you have full editorial control over (within the guidelines of the law) such as:

- Blogs
- Podcasts
- Events
- Books
- Video programming/films/documentaries
- Educational products

From social justice to sexual abuse, platforms driven by regular people are bringing a voice to the voiceless. Although unarmed African-Americans have been disproportionately killed by law enforcement since being kidnapped and brought to the US in chains, the nation didn't begin to have meaningful dialogue about the issue until #BlackLivesMatter created a platform for the conversation. dream hampton's documentary on the decades-long allegations of sexual abuse against singer R. Kelly not only led to new investigations into his behavior, but it also provided a space for communities to speak out against the ignored victimization of women at the hands of family members and acquaintances.

Platforms can organize scattered voices into a powerful force. Platforms can educate, enlighten and empower. And when platforms are driven by people that we like and trust, we can be inspired to change our lives and the world around us.

Isha Cogborn

PERSONAL BRAND + PLATFORM = IMPACT

If you've built a platform, but you're struggling to gain traction, chances are, there's a disconnect between who you are, who you want to help and what you're presenting to the world. Here are five strategies to help you build a more impactful platform:

1. **Check your ego at the door.**
   If you're doing this just to get attention, you're in it for the wrong reason. If you're doing it to prove all of the people who didn't believe in you wrong, your motivation is shrouded in negative energy. Ask yourself, "How do I want people to be better because they came in contact with me?" It's not about you. You're the pipe that greatness flows through to positively impact the lives of others.

> *It's not about trying to make everyone happy. It's about not unintentionally driving away the people we want to work with.*

2. **Know your audience.**
   One of the first questions I ask new clients is, "Who is your target audience?" If they say, "Everybody", then I know we have work to do. A key element of breaking through the noise and meaningfully connecting with your audience is knowing as much as possible about the people you want to reach. Traditionally, we've looked at demographics like age, gender, socioeconomic status and the like. But psychographics, defined by Merriam-Webster Dictionary as "market research or statistics classifying population groups according to psychological variables (such as attitudes, values, or fears)" are much more effective.

   If you're looking to help people solve a problem that

CHAPTER SEVENTEEN

you've solved for yourself, your best audience may be people who were like you. What challenges did you routinely face as a result of the problem? What was your motivation to fix it? What barriers stood between you and what you desired? How did the voices in your head and the people around you affect your progress?

By understanding where your target audience is, what they want and what they need, and by routinely speaking to it, your content will make them feel like you're walking around in their head. Wouldn't you rather listen to somebody who gets you specifically instead of speaking in broad, generic terms? When you try to reach everybody, you'll have a hard time reaching anybody.

> **It's not about you. You're the pipe that greatness flows through to positively impact the lives of others.**

3. **Pick your vehicle.**
   One of the greatest challenges people experience (including myself at times) is consistency. For years, my fear of inconsistency punked me out of starting a meetup group and launching a podcast. Then I realized that my 'on again, off again' ways were the consequence of biting off more than I could chew. If I didn't try to take on so much, I could be more consistent.

   Many marketing gurus will tell you that you need to be everywhere – blogging, YouTube, Facebook, LinkedIn, Instagram, podcasting, speaking, networking…are you tired yet? If you're committed to getting more than four hours of sleep each night, I challenge you to choose no more than two primary vehicles where you'll "live". This is the space where you'll share valuable content and build an engaged community. It could be a meetup group, online show, monthly webinars, or anything your target audience will find valuable and where they're likely to find you based on their lifestyle and habits. Being an early adopter on the latest emerging vehicle might seem like a good idea, but if your target audience isn't there yet, make sure you focus on growing your platform elsewhere, too.

Also look to vehicles that showcase your strengths. Do you have a vibrant and engaging personality? Video and speaking may serve you well. Would you rather put the spotlight on others? Consider a podcast.

4. **Find your voice.**
Curating content by sharing articles, videos and quotes from other experts can be an effective strategy. But if you want to be seen as a thought leader, you have to also tell your audience what you think. One of the fears that I help my clients overcome is feeling like they don't have anything new or valuable to say.

Here's a strategy to help you develop a fresh point of view:

Allow your brain to objectively process the information you receive instead of accepting it as truth – even if it's from a respected source. Has anything from your experiences provided you with a different perspective? What is missing from the conversation? Who is missing from the conversation? Dissenting from popular opinion can be scary, but it may be just what your audience needs. How can you give a voice to the voiceless?

Adopt a tone and style that allows your personality to shine through – even if you don't think it's particularly magnetic. This should go without saying, but actually communicate like a person. Unless your target audience is academic professionals, your content doesn't have to sound like a textbook. If your tribe is

CHAPTER SEVENTEEN

simply looking for information, a Google search will suffice. The way you serve up the information is what will get their attention and keep them coming back.

5. **Embrace imperfection.**
   As I talk to prospective collaborators for my Platform for Purpose Initiative, there are common fears and insecurities that arise

   "What if I mess up?"

   "I need to lose weight before I start making videos."

   "I don't like the way I look or sound on the air."

   "What if I don't get my content out on schedule?"

   "I don't know enough to be looked at as an expert."

   "What if someone disagrees with me?"

At the root, it all comes down to an unrealistic expectation of perfection. We feel like we have to do everything right and everyone needs to like us in order to make a difference. Let me take the pressure off of you with this newsflash: *You will never be perfect, and that's okay.*

In a world where every post is filtered and social media feeds are carefully curated, many audiences are placing greater value on transparency and imperfection. We want to hear from people who feel accessible and make us believe we can be like them, too.

Oprah Winfrey is easily the most recognizable media personality in the world. When national syndication of her television show began in the 80's, she was making the same "trash TV" as her counterparts on other networks. But then she decided to take us on her personal journey for a better life. She invited us to read the books she read and learn from the experts who changed her life. As a result, we became better… together. She shared her pain and struggles – from being sexually abused, challenges maintaining a healthy weight,

Isha Cogborn

and even secrets like developing a cocaine habit while in an emotionally abusive relationship. Oprah never pretended to be perfect or to have all of the answers. She simply invited us on a journey.

Instead of exhausting your energy on staged perfection, look for opportunities to invite your audience on a journey so that everyone can be better together.

ARE YOU READY TO OWN THE POWER OF YOUR PLATFORM?

Technology has gifted ordinary people with the unprecedented ability to make a difference in the world. If you have an overwhelming desire to reach people with your message, you don't have to be wealthy, you don't have to be wealthy, a supermodel or a Mensa-certified genius.. All it takes is clarity and commitment.

If you're ready to grow your purpose-driven platform, you don't have to do it alone. To download your free guide, Personal Branding On Purpose, visit **www.MyBrandOnPurpose.com**

CONCLUSION

Do you feel like there's something greater that you were put on earth to accomplish? Are you tired of accepting the status quo as the best that life has to offer? If you have read the past 17 chapters, I know the gap has been closed between you and your best life.

Ten years ago, I had a successful corporate career, made great money and lived a respectable middle-class life, but I wasn't happy. I felt like a hamster trapped on a golden wheel, longing for a greater sense of meaning. When I discovered by purpose, it was like seeing the world through a new set of eyes. My purpose became the fuel that gets me out of bed in the morning when I want to hit snooze. It helps me to put what can feel like life-shattering setbacks into perspective. Knowing my purpose leads me to always look for the lesson: What can I take from this to help someone else?

If you haven't discovered your purpose, I hope this book sparked your desire to figure it out. If you're out of alignment with your purpose, you'll go through your entire life feeling like something is missing. No matter how big your house is, how nice your car is, or how many designer clothes you own, nothing will be able to fill the void. You don't have to continue to live in misery or uncertainty and that's why we wrote this book for you.

I meet so many talented, purpose-driven people with knowledge and wisdom that can light up your entire world. That's why I created the **Platform for Purpose Initiative**. As you learn more about our journey and connect with us outside of the pages of this book, you'll see we're regular people who experience some of the same challenges that have been holding you back.

The road wasn't easy for any of us, but we kept going.

You can, too.

The world is full of people with passions they never pursued. Great ideas they never followed up on. Incredible visions they never even uttered. If you have a vision in your heart that won't go away, it's there for a reason. Don't give up on it just because other people can't see what you see or because you don't feel qualified to achieve it. By ignoring it, you're not only depriving yourself of unimaginable joy and fulfillment, but you also rob the world of your greatness.

This is not about you. It's about what you have to offer those you were created to serve.

If you need help living your best life, send me (*Isha Cogborn*) a message at **Isha@EpiphanyInstitute.com**.

Made in the USA
Columbia, SC
23 August 2019